UTILITARIANISM AND ALL THAT

Books by
RAGHAVAN IYER

Parapolitics: Toward the City of Man
The Glass Curtain
Utilitarianism and All That
Novus Ordo Seclorum
The Jewel in the Lotus

RAGHAVAN IYER is Professor of Political Science at the University of California, Santa Barbara. Educated in Bombay and at Oxford, he was a Rhodes Scholar and President of the Oxford Union. He taught political philosophy at Oxford for eight years and was a Visiting Professor at the Universities of Oslo, Ghana and Chicago. He was a Consultant to the Fund for the Republic and a member of the Club of Rome and the Reform Club. He is President of the Institute of World Culture and the Pythagorean Academy.

UTILITARIANISM AND ALL THAT

Utilitarianism and All That deftly unravels the main strands of British imperial policy in India from Hastings to Attlee. It begins by examining, in principle and practice, the Burkean theory of trusteeship, the Benthamite concern with the use of power, the assumption of a quasi-Platonic role as benevolent guardians, and the recurrent sense of an evangelical mission. It also shows the interactions and inversions of these strands, woven around nationalist responses to imperial policies. Beyond its application to Britain and India, *Utilitarianism and All That* provides a basis for understanding inequity in international relations, and offers penetrating insights into the origins and prospects of the post-colonial world. This brilliant work, first published by Chatto & Windus, London, in 1960, has already become an international classic.

UTILITARIANISM
AND ALL THAT

THE POLITICAL THEORY OF
BRITISH IMPERIALISM

RAGHAVAN IYER

CONCORD GROVE PRESS
1983

INSTITUTE OF WORLD CULTURE
&
CONCORD GROVE PRESS
London   *Santa Barbara*   *New York*

Copyright © 1983 Raghavan N. Iyer
First Printing: October 2, 1983

ISBN 0-88695-003-1

Printed in the United States of America

In memory of

SIR MAURICE GWYER
T. D. WELDON
F. W. DEAKIN
LORD PETHICK-LAWRENCE
GUY WINT

CONTENTS

UTILITARIANISM AND ALL THAT

The political phraseology of the English in India is the same as the political phraseology of our countrymen at home. But it is never to be forgotten that the same words stand for very different things in London and at Calcutta. . . .

THOMAS MACAULAY

Is a governor in India to consult Puffendorf and Grotius? No. But I will tell you what he is to consult; the laws of nature — not the statutes to be found in those books, nor in any books — but those laws which are to be found in Europe, Africa and Asia, that are to be found amongst all mankind, those principles of equity and humanity implanted in our hearts which have their existence in the feelings of mankind that are capable of judging.

CHARLES FOX

1

GUILT AND ATONEMENT

It has long been an accepted part of the apologetics of modern imperialism to invoke the analogy and the precedent of the Roman Empire. More especially, the comparison has often been made of the role of the British in India and of the Romans in Greece. The Romans and the British, it was plausibly argued, were uniquely able to confer peace and order, law and justice, on the peoples they conquered. They were historic instruments of cultural diffusion and political unification and thus rendered an undeniable service even to ancient, self-contained civilizations that were no less advanced than their own. If Lucullus and Dalhousie indulged the appetite for aggressive, expanding imperialism, there were also those like Cato and Cobden, Scipio and Bright, who were averse to an indefinite extension of the area of imperial responsibility. The Romans were better able than the British to assimilate their imperial subjects and to bring them, regardless of race or colour, into the ambit of a common citizenship. The British, on the other hand, were more enlightened than the Romans in their conceptions of the liberty of the subject and the rule of law.

Both were convinced that they had far more to give

than to receive and tended to conceive of their civilizing mission in messianic terms. In this regard there were rare examples of cultural tolerance and humility among the Romans as well as the British. Cicero, for instance, wrote to his brother Quintus, who was governor of Asia in 60 B.C., that "we are set over a race of men who not only possess the higher culture, but are held to be the source from which it has spread to others". A retired British civil servant of India wrote in 1926 that considerations of racial inequality between rulers and ruled were quite irrelevant. "What race is there should claim superiority to peoples that gave the world a Buddha, an Asoka and an Akbar, religions and philosophies that embrace every religion that has ever existed, an epic literature perhaps unrivalled, and some of the greatest masterpieces in the realm of human art?" And yet, there was a consensus of opinion that the *gravitas* of the true Roman and of the true Briton gave them a title to rule, almost amounting to a divine right, that was lacking in the frivolous and slothful Levantine Greek as well as in the soft and indolent Indian, who was regarded even by Burke as "approaching almost to feminine tenderness". This posture of political condescension could assume absurd proportions and sometimes sink to despicable and dangerous levels. But it was in no way comparable to the crude, cruel bigotry of the Spanish Catholic colonists who have been described as "reckless, ruthless, like men intoxicated".

The similarities with the Roman Empire, actual and alleged, cannot do as much credit to the British

Empire as its overriding dissimilarity in one crucial respect — the sense of guilt and the desire for atonement. There was a gnawing doubt from the first that could not be quelled by the passion for fanfare and pride in grandeur that reached their climax under Curzon. As the Oxford classicist, Edwyn Bevan, noticed at the time, the vulgar revelry in vastitude of conquest and even the plea of national self-interest could never satisfy the British rulers as a justification of their Indian empire. As long as the sense of guilt was irrepressible, the self-conscious urge for justification was also inescapable. Outside England, the insistence on moral idealism rather than on material advantage appeared to be either a feeble form of self-deception or a flagrant example of national hypocrisy. How could the sincere moral protestations of English defenders of empire be appreciated by those foreigners who never had a Puritan Revolution and who were never persecuted by their own high principles?

What better for men burdened by moral doubts than to disavow considerations of narrow self-interest or shallow grandeur and to invoke the utilitarian creed as an unanswerable justification? Could it not be argued that the British Empire was uniquely useful to the Indian masses, a self-evident fact that was denied by the Indian intelligentsia (those benighted Brahmin 'Baboos' and their 'crafty' Bania leaders) only because of their innate dishonesty or their neurotic narcissism? To the question "What right here gave its sanction to might?", surely a ruling race could answer, in all sincerity, in terms of its solemn duty to serve the interests of the ruled and to

protect them from their own weaknesses and the designs
of ambitious men who exploit the emotions of others
for their own ends. Such an answer at any rate comes
naturally to those who are sufficiently developed morally
to admit, in the first place, that there is a question to be
answered.

Today, more than ever before, the utilitarian plea
comes in handy as an *ex post facto* justification. It is
now fortunately unfashionable to talk openly of the
civilizing mission of the white races, of the sacred
responsibilities of self-appointed, Platonic guardians or
even the austere and tedious tasks of trusteeship assumed
as a result of the accidents of history if not as an act of
providence. In the early phase of the acquirement of
power, its instrumental value is stressed. As power
becomes concentrated in a settled ruling class and
exercised through recognized institutions and procedures,
it tends to become a self-justifying phenomenon. The
fact that it is such a vital element in the pursuit of other
and even laudable goals tends to transform its very
nature. When power is lost, or when it is shed, it cannot
be retrospectively justified as an autonomous value which
is somehow identified with all other values that are
deemed worthwhile. It must be seen entirely as an
instrumental value that is judged solely by its fruits. The
temptation is strong to explain away, or to conceal, or
to deny, past tendencies to pursue it beyond all other
values. This temptation has been splendidly resisted by
Professor Thornton in his *The Imperial Idea and Its
Enemies.*

Further, it can clearly be shown, as has been brilliantly done by Professor Stokes in his *English Utilitarians and India,* that utilitarianism is not just a convenient device of imperialist self-defence on meeting its end. It was actually the deliberate policy of a gifted and eccentric ruling class in those formative years before the Crown took over from the Company full responsibility for the government of the Indian subcontinent. It can, therefore, be all the more easily fitted into an elegant Whig-Imperialist model often used by hacks to celebrate, not merely justify, the record of British rule in Asia. The British not only transmitted to an alien, Asiatic people the spirit of the European Renaissance and of the Reformation and the Enlightenment. They not only extended an aristocratic Establishment from an island to a global empire. They also exported the Age of Reform from Liberal England, the virtues of public probity and State philanthropy, and the magic carpet of collectivism in harmony with private enterprise to an underdeveloped continent in its pre-industrial state of nature.

The government of India was regarded at times as "not only a government but the chief landlord", as "an improving proprietor on an enormous scale". British rule had to "play the part of universal provider and special providence". To cap it all, the British were not only responsible for "the introduction in the midst of Brahmins of European views of the universe". They also gave away the secret weapons of petitioning authority and even of engineering a relatively bloodless revolution. Just as voters worked for the voteless, Christians for the emancipation of the Jews, masters for the abolition of slavery and Protestants for the emancipation of the Catholics, so the British helped to free their subjects from their political slavery. All this special pleading is perfectly understandable and makes enough sense of the facts to become the basis of popular political mythology today. If nationalists, on the other side, need to rewrite history along Promethean lines of continuous, determined revolt against absolute tyranny, if they need to meet every plea of expediency with the sovereign talisman of the natural rights of all men under the universal sway of natural law, imperialist writers on their side require the holy name of Utility to provide a further *raison d'être* for Raison d'Etat. And so the debate goes on, from the British Empire of yesterday to the diverse neo-colonialist games of our own day.

2

THEORY AND PRACTICE

The appeal from imperialism to utilitarianism has interesting consequences not only for appreciating Indo-British relations and modern imperial history, but also for a study of liberal political theory and the two faces of utilitarianism. Utilitarian considerations are not merely the basis of representative democracy and liberal capitalism. They can also be equally employed to justify authoritarian regimes and enlightened, benevolent despotism. Interference with the negative liberties of others is not only justifiable (rightly or wrongly) in terms of idealistic metaphysics and occult references to higher selves and real wills. It could also be defended in terms of the 'real' and long-term interests of others that may be unknown to them. Negative liberty itself, the area within which a man can do what he wants, may equally be justified by the utilitarian argument that a man needs the licence to do what he wants as by a purer moral plea that a man's power of choice is somehow sacred and, therefore, inalienable.

Once, however, the utilitarian element enters into the notion of liberty, the danger of justifiable coercion arises in a subtle manner through the argument that a man may be trained how to choose and how to know what his needs and all his wants are. More generally and more plausibly, an imperialist could claim that he can protect the negative liberties of his subjects better than they could do by themselves or through representatives of their own race and nationality. It is not, therefore, surprising that the nationalist has to retaliate against a theory of authoritarian utilitarianism by producing a theory of transferred natural rights, *i.e.,* by basing the sanctity of individual personality on its supposed connection with national status.

The abuse of notions of positive liberty, general will and higher selves is not peculiar to them. The fact that it is more common is only because these notions have a wider political currency and a greater moral force. Seminal political concepts are interdependent and interdefinable. We can only anathematize the most vulnerable concepts by taking a partial and incomplete view of political theory itself. Such a course is open to the critic but not to the creator of political systems, although the critic can point to the special and dispensable presuppositions that the great system-builders assume without question to be absolute. Utilitarianism, like every original and powerful political doctrine, can be and has been invoked on behalf of authority as well as freedom, as a theory of government as well as a theory of society. It not merely recognized each man's right to seek his own happiness but also championed the duty of the state to produce, by deliberate and systematic interference, a harmony of interests. It incorporated the element of benevolence stressed by Hutcheson as well as the element of coercion and even of ruthlessness by means of which Hobbes pushed utilitarian ideas to totalitarian extremes. The young Bentham was an advocate of enlightened despotism and never became a wholehearted democrat. The elder Mill believed that happiness and not liberty was the end of government. He formulated in its extreme form the absurdly extravagant doctrine of 'oriental despotism' which provided an alibi for the translation of British utilitarianism into the theory and policy of imperialism in India. His son's passionate concern for liberty led him to assert that it was impossible for one people to govern another. At the same time, the influence of his father's *History of India* made him deny the applicability of his theories of liberty and of representative government to the conditions prevalent in Eastern dependencies. Although he felt himself at a great distance from his father's "tone of thought and feeling", he found that they were "almost always in strong agreement on the political questions of the day". He also found many points of sympathy between him and Austin, who "never ceased to be a utilitarian" and thought that "there was more practical good government under the Prussian monarchy than under the English representative government".

The authoritarian element in British utilitarianism easily lent itself to serve imperialist ends as well as imperialist theories of self-justification. Imperialist experience in its turn further weakened and sometimes destroyed the feeling for the liberal element in utilitarianism. To Milner, both the British Constitution and the party system were "antiquated and bad", as they undermined the effectiveness of positive government. To Fitzjames Stephen, who was more Hobbesian than Bentham or Austin, John Stuart Mill had perverted the pure doctrine of his father by yoking it to popular liberalism. The task of government was to impose the ideal of happiness of a gifted ruling class upon a passive majority that had to be saved from all anarchic tendencies. But such ideas, like the earlier nabobs and the latter-day sahibs who returned to England, were strangers in the land of their birth. Apart from the liberal heritage of the past, the rising power of the middle classes was hostile in an era of expanding trade to autocratic and bureaucratic government. Liberty at home could thus coexist with despotism abroad.

The expansion of England required a compromise between conflicting principles that the country could well afford. Disraeli's formula, *Imperium et Libertas,* left it open whether empire or liberty was to be the ruling principle and the dominant theme in English life, although Disraeli preferred the former, for it was "as selfish as patriotism". Even Gladstone, who could become ecstatic about liberty, thought that "the sentiment of empire may be called innate in every Briton. If there are exceptions, they are like those of men born blind or lame among us. It is part of our patrimony: born with our birth, dying only with our death; incorporating itself in the first elements of our knowledge, and interwoven with all our habits of mental action upon public affairs."*

It is possible to argue that if we are justified in condemning Rousseau by Robespierre, Hegel by Hitler and Marx by Stalin, we are also entitled to judge Bentham by Bentinck, Burke by Curzon and the two Mills by those who invoked the notion of 'oriental despotism' to oppose every demand for political progress in India. The search for scapegoats whose crucifixion can atone for monstrous systems of error and evil is itself based, however, on an unduly rationalistic faith in the influence of theory and on an absurdly simple view of both individual and national character. Herder may have good reason to assert that a history of opinions would really be the key to the history of deeds. It is, however, one thing to stress the impact of ideas and opinions on policies and actions. It is quite another matter to single out certain thinkers or theories or concepts as responsible for what they could neither have visualized nor intended in all its implications. The history of ideas is, as Meinecke so clearly saw, "no mere shadow-play or sequence of grey theories; on the contrary, it is the life-blood of events, absorbed into the life-blood of those men who are called upon to express the essential element of their epoch". In pleading against the tyrannical and tragic consequences of isms and systems, we may foist too easily the entire burden of blame upon those very thinkers whose theories were most vulnerable to distortion as well as exploitation.

* "England's Mission", *The Nineteenth Century*, September 1878.

Political theories may be rejections as well as rationalizations of features of national tradition. Political thinkers may revolt against prevalent social conditions and political forms and practices, either because of nostalgia or utopianism, anarchistic discontent or optimism, or because they cannot comprehend the social forces of their time. They are as much the product of their national tradition and temperament as those who use and abuse their theories in later epochs, or while they are still alive. The subtle connection between ideas and acts, theories and policies, as well as between ideas and excuses, theories and slogans, can be reduced to a stark simplicity if we take a monistic view of human motive and adopt a harsh certainty with regard to human nature, if we are too behaviouristic and too deterministic in our approach. The ideas as well as the intentions behind any system of power should not, however, be regarded as good or evil *per se*. We can never be clear or certain enough to draw up an indictment (or a panegyric) against a whole people, or even against an entire ruling class.

The over-estimation of theory as well as the over-simplification of ideas and intentions must especially be safeguarded against in the case of the British, who have ever been improvisers *par excellence*. It is not merely that inconsistency of character and absence of definite aim are most notably Anglo-Saxon qualities, as Cromer thought. It is not so much that the Englishman has no general ideas, as Dilke asserted. Nor is it just that the English governing class has more highly developed than any other a sense of the possible and has an almost prophetic knowledge of when it is necessary to retreat. The late André Siegfried came closest to the heart of the matter when he said* that the Englishman acts like an old-time sailor who manoeuvres in an unstable environment and who believes that Nature does not allow man to meet every contingency with ready-made, tidy solutions. Further, the Protestant Englishman, unlike the Catholic Frenchman, assumes personal responsibility for his actions and feels the need for atonement rather than for absolution, because it is with his own conscience and sense of duty that he must settle his affairs. For this reason, perhaps, the Englishman sometimes became almost insensitive to the feelings of others and behaved imperially like a Victorian nanny. J.S. Mill attributes his father's deficiency in tenderness to his being English. Henri Bourassa, the French-Canadian nationalist, complained that in spite of his remarkable faculties for government, and the general humanity of his proceedings, the Anglo-Saxon did not know how to gain the confidence, much less the affection, of the peoples that he dominated. It is, however, easy to create an Aunt Sally out of English national character.

It is absurd to read too much into English history and to assert that the Englishman is anti-revolutionary because he is too dull to take in a great idea and too selfish to apply it to any interest save his own. It may well be, as a contemporary English socialist has argued, that "the picture given by British political theorists of 'man

* *The Character of Peoples*, Chapter 4.

the political animal' belies at every point the British political animal. The former is a cool and calculating hedonist, bound by no ties which self-interest cannot justify; the latter is a sentimentalist, content to accept ancestral institutions and modify them to existing circumstances according to the mysterious canons of fair play." It is certainly true that the Englishman, whilst willing to display abroad his talent for compromise and conciliation to a lesser extent than at home, was tempted to experiment in the colonies with theories that were distrusted in practice in his own country. But even here it is possible to argue that the actual policies were of less importance in some cases than the particular men whom we praise or blame for implementing them in their own peculiar way.

3

ATTITUDES TO EMPIRE

The British Empire in India was, of course, *sui generis*. It still seems incredible that a handful of Englishmen could rule an alien and ancient civilization of many millions over a vast and varied subcontinent for over a century with a mixture of motives and methods, policies and principles, that baffles analysis and defies explanation. Mill said in his *Autobiography* that no government had, on the whole, given so much proof, to the extent of its lights, of good intention towards its subjects. And yet, Munro could write as early as 1818 to Hastings: "Foreign conquerors have treated the natives with violence, and often with great cruelty, but none has treated them with so much scorn as we." Macaulay proclaimed in 1833 that the Indian Empire, "the strangest of all political anomalies", resembled no other in history and formed by itself a separate class of political phenomena so that its growth and decay were regulated by unknown laws. It could certainly be contended that the "unnatural connection" between England and India was the result of some abnormality in India rather than in England. The brightest jewel in the Crown was at no time nearly as important to England as the politics of the nearby European states. England, which had valiantly resisted Spanish imperialism in the sixteenth century, French imperialism in the nineteenth century and German imperialism in the twentieth century, could never become deeply agitated about its own imperialism in India.

Within India itself, the spiritual and cultural exclusiveness of the Hindu and the social and intellectual aloofness of the English fostered a gulf between rulers and ruled that seemed to be unbridgeable and only to grow rather than to narrow with the passage of time. The sense of alienation was at all times overpowering and total in its nature except for a fortunate few. Most of them could cross the cultural barrier only by losing their own roots, by tearing themselves away from the tyranny of caste on either side. Despite the petty prejudices of men, the historical forces released by the Indo-British connection were of enormous magnitude and enduring significance. India unwittingly facilitated the Industrial Revolution in England and England unwillingly stimulated the Indian Renaissance. The inevitable clash and involuntary contact between races and between cultures were almost cosmic in their effects, for Asia and Europe never met so fruitfully since the ephemeral expedition to India of Alexander of Macedon. The results of the British encounter with India may yet prove to be more far-reaching and even deeper than the consequences of the Roman Empire.

The mid-Victorian Radicals in England were deeply concerned about the consequences of the Empire for their own country as well as for the helpless colonies, and protested against the prevalent mood of casual complacency. Cobden could see no advantage either to the natives or to their foreign masters in this vast Indian possession and was aware that "a feeling of alienation was constantly increasing with both the natives and the English". Furthermore, if a Board of Works could not give a common sewer for London, was it likely to cover India with canals for irrigation? If Catholic and Protestant could not live together peacefully in Belfast, were the British the people to teach Christian charity to the Hindus? The British had adopted in India "the principle of a military despotism" and such an undertaking could only be "a calamity and a curse to the people of England". Bright was bothered about the cost of governing India and the meagre sums spent upon its people compared to the "monstrous" salaries paid to British officials. The edifice reared was too vast for management and there was no man competent to govern the whole of India. If India were to be governed for the good of England, the good of England must come through the channels of the good of India, and India must become rich in order that England may become rich.

If India were to be governed and not to be abandoned, "calumny" against Indians must cease. They had the highest claims on their rulers who must recognize that there was a judgement for nations as for individuals. There was a higher and holier glory than military conquest and that could come through conferring solid and lasting benefits upon the Indian people. The system of government had to be changed, for "what would be thought if the whole of Europe was under one governor, who knew only the language of the Feejee Islands?" If they retained the "fatal gift of empire" without the ability to govern it, finally India would be avenged. If, on the other hand, they were willing to prepare for the time when India will have to take up her own government, they would be "endeavouring to make amends for the original crime upon which much of our power in India is founded, and for the many mistakes which have been made by men whose intentions have been good". The Radicals were voices in the wilderness. Their influence was not immediate or obvious, their ideas were never consciously or fully carried out. Yet they provided one element in British imperialism in India that was muted, but never wholly discarded. The concept of atonement lingered till the Empire came to its end, under the auspices of Attlee.

Other elements were, however, more to the fore most of the time. There was the noble Roman element, the desire to maintain the rule of law and to cherish the *pax Britannica,* the sheer concern for good government in the most earthy sense but on a grand scale. This was well expressed by the Earl of Mayo in his address at Ajmere in 1869 to the princes and chiefs of Rajputana. He then pleaded "that justice and order shall prevail, that every man's property shall be secure, that the traveller shall come and go in safety, that the cultivator shall enjoy the fruits of his labours, and the trader the produce of his commerce: that you shall make roads, and undertake the construction of those works of irrigation which will improve the condition of the people and swell the revenues of your states: that you shall encourage education and provide for the relief of the sick".

There was also the exclusive Semitic element, the calm belief that the English were the elect, divinely appointed to bear the white man's burden for the benefit of those beyond the pale. This was proclaimed most clearly by Disraeli, easily combined with the prevailing notions of political Darwinism, and later on popularized by Kipling. "Progress and reaction", declared Disraeli, "are but words . . . all is race." In *Coningsby* he said that "Toryism indeed is but copied from the mighty prototype which has fashioned Europe." In *Lord George Bentinck* he observed that the Jews are the trustees of tradition, "a living and the most striking evidence of the falsity of that pernicious doctrine of modern times, the natural equality of man". He was profoundly convinced of the inherent superiority of English, as of Jewish, blood, and the consequent righteousness of making a Promised Land of the territory of others. His conception of the British Empire had a magical glow for those who were within the charmed circle. If England was to maintain her empire, she must come to believe in her uniqueness so completely that other peoples — at any rate in her dependent territories — would come to believe it as well. For him, colonies possessed intrinsic and not merely instrumental value. Even in 1866, when Chancellor of the Exchequer, he had written that "power and influence we should exercise in Asia; consequently in Eastern Europe, consequently also in Western Europe". The Empire needed its loyal believers and champions. The climax of emotion came when Queen Victoria was proclaimed Empress of India in 1877.

Further, there was the aggressive Prussian element, the pride in military power, the deification of discipline, the requirement of docility in the ruled, the justification of brutality and violence to overthrow militant opposition to the regime. This element was rather rare but it did exist, especially at intermediate levels of the hierarchy. It was partially expressed by Michael O'Dwyer, Governor of the Punjab, who defended General Dyer's action at Amritsar, and who condemned Montagu for his "sentimental, futile and humiliating policy". He had no use for the Congress which created disaffection among the simple and credulous masses and he was in favour of crushing "the insidious campaign of Peaceful Rebellion". He quoted with approval Churchill's statement in 1930 that "Gandhism and all it stands for will sooner or later have to be grappled with and finally crushed. It is of no use trying to satisfy a tiger with scraps of cat's meat." He wanted a policy of "firmness" rather than of "vague idealism" and felt that the Parliament must be "of more robust spirit" and not "the slave of catchwords and slogans" which would lead it to throw away "our great Indian Empire, the greatest achievement of the British race".

British imperialism in India was thus compounded of

diverse and even contradictory elements, the chief of which were the Roman (or Asokan or Buddhist) element of peace under law; the Semitic (or Brahmin) element of racial exclusiveness and destiny; the Prussian (or Moghul or Kautilyan) element of militancy and firmness; and the nonconformist Radical (or Christian or Hindu) element of atonement and penance and expiation. These elements were embodied in the principles of government, the men who were selected to carry the burden of administration, and the institutional structure of the imperial system. The principles reflected the aims and needs of a just but alien, a firm but not conscienceless, despotism. The governing class was a proud and exclusive caste, conscious of its political and military power, anxious to preserve the peace and to maintain the rule of law, occasionally troubled by moral qualms or mental doubts. The system consisted of a centralized judiciary and police force, a narrowly based and well-bred civil service, a powerful state with a competent intelligence wing and a disciplined army, and a slow extension of minimal opportunities for the expression of public grievances and moderate opposition to the government. It is important to keep some sort of balance between the relative roles of the personalities who constituted the ruling class, the theories that influenced their policies, and the system which was set up and acquired in time a distinctive shape and decisive significance.

Curzon may have been right in stating that "Government goes by personality." But when he pleaded in his farewell speech to the Byculla Club that "one-man

supervision is the very best form of government,
presuming the man to be competent", and that the only
alternative was "a most mechanical and lifeless"
bureaucracy, he was, in fact, voicing a particular theory
of centralized, personal rule that others disliked. A
reaction was bound to set in. After all, even the doctrines
of German idealism before 1800 acquired political
significance only in the Prussian bureaucracy. The
servants of the Crown embraced "seditious ideas" and
invoked the liberal principles of Kant to undermine
the soulless rigour and intolerant oppressiveness of
Frederick's rulership. Individual freedom to think, the
right to dissent, became "the gateway to professional
happiness, to self-disciplined discretionary action . . . and
to the replacement of erratic dynastic autocracy by a
more magnanimous and more efficient form of despotic
government, by humanized bureaucratic absolutism,
'which will find it advantageous to itself to treat man,
who thenceforth is more than a machine, in accord with
his dignity' ".* Many apologists for the British Empire
would prefer to argue that bad theories were applied by
good administrators than *vice versa*. They would even
like to think that the theories as well as the men who
applied (or modified or ignored) them were good rather
then bad, taking everything into account.

Philip Woodruffe has invoked the Christian maxim that
men should be judged by their best rather than by their

* Hans Rosenberg, *Bureaucracy, Democracy and Autocracy*, 1958, p.
189.

worst and presumably also rejects the apparently Semitic belief that theories should be judged by their worst rather than by their best applications. It would indeed be a counsel of perfection to demand that we must always judge all men and all theories after taking their best as well as their worst acts and applications into full consideration. But, surely, we must at least maintain levels of consistency and fairness that are required both by true intellectual standards and by all religious teaching. If we wish to judge men by their best, we must do so with nationalists as well as with imperialists and *vice versa,* which the followers of no religion find easy to do. If we wish to judge theories by their worst formulations and results, we must do so with those which appeal to us as well as with those which annoy us from the start, which intellectuals of all types find easier to attempt than to achieve.

There is clearly something to be said for an examination of the theories involved in British government in India. They are at least less difficult to detect than the complex motives that governed the conduct of the varied men who made up an entire ruling class. If nothing else is gained, we can at any rate try to prevent the enthroning of a particular theory or school of thinkers as the chief determinant over a century of foreign rule. In the twenties Huxley commented on the haphazard oscillation between contrary theories that was dictated by the changing circumstances of British rule in India.

Old and new strangely coexist, and India is ruled in

accordance with two completely incompatible theories of
government: that of Akbar, shall we say, and that of
Woodrow Wilson. On Monday the watchword of the
executive is 'Reform and responsible self-government'; like
Oliver Twist the Indians immediately ask for more: their
demands become increasingly insistent, and the Government
nervously decides to be firm. On Tuesday some General
Dyer rivals the exploits of the Moghuls; repressive legislation
is passed, and the gaols are crowded. On Wednesday the
Government is seized with qualms. Remembering what Mr.
Gladstone said in 1882 and why the Great War was fought, it
makes a 'generous gesture'. The response is so unenthusiastic
that it becomes necessary on Thursday to suspend the
Habeas Corpus Act and imprison several thousand subjects
without a trial. By the end of the week everybody, including
the Government itself, is feeling rather muddled.

Jesting Pilate

The state of muddle was even more complicated over
the entire period of British rule in India. There were, at
least, four distinct strands – the Burkean doctrine of
imperial trusteeship, the utilitarian theory of state
activity that was propounded mainly by Bentham but
also by the two Mills, the Platonic conception of a
ruling élite that would act as wise guardians, and the
Evangelical zeal to spread the gospel so as to elevate the
character and save the souls of even perversely unwilling
people. Each of these strands had several aspects and
assumed a variety of forms, with differing degrees of
theoretical purity and practical debasement. The pure
Burkean doctrine was distorted, especially at times of
stress, by the Prussian element in imperialism so that the
solemn trustees could become overbearing and even
oppressive. They were sometimes translated into petty

tyrants of whom Burke would never have approved. The Benthamite doctrine could degenerate into Hobbesian coercion and concentration of power, but it was also sublimated by the Roman element in British imperialism into a theory of legal unification and state philanthropy. The Platonic doctrine was sometimes enhanced by a Whig belief in liberalism and in progress, but it was also pathetically perverted to the point of caricature by the Semitic element in British imperialism which gave the concept of the chosen race. The Evangelical doctrine gave rise to many religious fears and resentments among the Indian people, but it was fortunately counterbalanced by the nonconformist Radical element in British imperialism, by the Christian notion of atonement which required that a believer should not neglect his own sins while saving the souls of brethren beyond the pale.

The Burkean doctrine could be used to support the view that the British had greatness thrust upon them. The Benthamite doctrine could show that Britain could become great by her activities abroad. The Platonic doctrine could be taken to mean that the British were born great, with an innate right to rule over others. The Evangelical doctrine could be used to assert that the greatness to be sought and secured was not of this world and lay far in the future, as a reward for present efforts to extend the influence on earth of the divine word and the divine will. The trustees had to take 'oriental stagnation' for granted and to display a profound distrust of the new Indian intelligentsia, from whom the varied peasantry and their ancestral traditions had to be protected. The utilitarians were saved from disturbing doubts about their own policies by the bogey of 'oriental despotism' and by their belief in the need for social reform and popular education. The guardians had to remind themselves continually about 'oriental backwardness' and the inferiority of the Indian ruling class which was nearing its natural demise, leaving the rest in the position of Peter Pan. The Peter Pan theory of India, as J.A. Spender called it, was compounded by two separate ideas — the East is unchanging and Orientals are like children. The evangelicals took for granted that 'oriental superstition and vice' could not be met by anything in Indian religious tradition, as they were directly and causally connected. A policy of non-interference or of toleration of Indian religions was solely a matter of temporary expediency and even an invitation to divine vengeance, which came in the form of the Mutiny.

Besides the four chief strands of theory, there were no doubt minor elements derived from Aristotle, Locke, Austin, T.H. Green, Spencer and Buckle and several others. But the influence of these was intermittent and limited in scope and in their applicability to the central problem of imperial government in India. The Burkean, Benthamite, Platonic and Evangelical doctrines were useful for imperial administration as well as apologetics. They could be made the basis of a theory of government, a theory of society and a theory of history which were adaptable to the needs of a highly centralized system of benevolent and durable despotism over an alien, vast and diverse population in a distant subcontinent.

4

BURKEAN TRUSTEESHIP

All empire is power in trust", said Dryden in *Absalom and Achitophel.* Nowhere has this concept been so clearly stated as in the speeches of Burke. In his celebrated oration on Fox's India Bill in 1783, Burke asserted that government is "in the strictest sense a trust". All political power set over men and all privileges claimed against the natural equality of mankind ought to be some way or other exercised ultimately for their benefit. Further, "it is of the very essence of every trust to be rendered accountable, and even totally to cease, when it substantially varies from the purposes for which alone it could have a lawful existence". Trustees had "no right to make a market" of their duties. If a trust held derivatively is abused, "the contract is broken" and the holders of the trust originally re-enter into all their rights, *i.e.*, into the exercise of all their duties. Parliament had no sort of "epicurean excuse to stand aloof". British governors ought to "govern on British principles, not by British forms", said Burke five years later, calling for a spirit of equity, justice, protection and "lenity" and attacking the notion of "geographical morality". At the same time he pleaded against forcing on others "the narrow circle of our ideas" regarding custom and usage.

He insisted that oriental governments know nothing of arbitrary power even if the British have better institutions for the preservation of the rights of men than any other country in the world. In Asia as in Europe "the same law of nations prevails", the same political principles and maxims are "continually resorted to" and "strenuously maintained". Burke took pains to examine "the constitution of oriental governments" and came to the view that "Asia is enlightened in that respect as well as Europe". No one in modern Europe has more stoutly spurned the facile aspersion of 'oriental despotism'. He displayed an imagination and a tolerance lacking in liberals like Macaulay. Burke was more anxious to reform the English trustees in India than their numerous subjects with their ancient beliefs and diverse customs, "a people for ages civilized and cultivated; cultivated by all the arts of polished life, while we were yet in the woods". He was against every form of "social engineering" or "political geometry" which sprang from the Jacobin simplification of man. He believed that circumstances give to every political principle "its distinguishing colour and discriminating effect". But Burke had a notion of government and of trusteeship which required that human wants should be provided for by human wisdom, even against individual as well as collective inclinations. He could go as far as to say that "the restraints on men, as well as their liberties, are to be reckoned among their rights".

There was even a proprietary as well as a contractual element in Burke's notion of government; the rights of government were almost a form of private ownership. 'State' and 'Estate' were almost identical so that public and private affairs could not be sharply differentiated. It is not surprising that Burke's social philosophy and his notion of history were behind the outlook of men like Munro, Malcolm, Metcalfe, and Elphinstone. The conception of benevolent landlordism combined a Benthamite theory of government with a Burkean view of society. Social conservatism was wedded for a time to a liberal spirit of reform.

The Burkean doctrine of trusteeship was common to conservatives and to liberals, although their differences as to the period of transition and the policies to be followed were serious enough not to be wholly obscured by the illusion of permanency that they both began to share. Even the radicals were influenced by the doctrine of trusteeship, although they had their fears about its feasibility. The natives, said Bright, were like sheep without a shepherd. The doctrine remained, however, essentially conservative, for it usually went with a reverence for the past, a distrust of theory, an organic conception of society, a feeling for constitutional continuity, a stress upon loyalty and *esprit de corps,* a concern with duties rather than with rights, a belief in the complexity of human nature and in the secondary importance of politics, a love of fox-hunting ("the wisest religion", as Quintin Hogg called it), the dream of a *Civitas Dei* distinct from the political system, the acceptance of a religious basis for civil society and the view that all universal ideas must be modified in terms

of common sense and expediency so as to allow for
what Disraeli called "the necessities of nations".

Burke wanted the trustees to be "faithful watchmen"
over the rights and privileges of the people, whilst he had
no use for what Coleridge later on condemned as the
"talismanic influence" of legislation. Burke is really not
the philosopher of British conservatism alone, but of
British political life from Right to Left, especially when
projected abroad. Gladstone, Ramsay MacDonald and
Lansbury all took for granted the deep organic
conservatism of British social life. Despite the language
of interest and reason and the preaching of utilitarianism,
the imperial ruling class, with its continuity of tradition
and fluidity of membership, cherished in practice the
fragile bonds of collective sentiment and conscience and
evolved their own handy notions of what constituted
'the rules of the game' and 'fair play'.

The doctrine of trusteeship was taken seriously
even to the extent that in practice it meant an
unwillingness to delegate responsibility and to trust the
natives to do anything for themselves. The trustees
assumed that they alone loved and knew the *real* India,
and what began as an underestimation of the new Indian
intelligentsia became in time a fierce phobia. References
were made to the "oriental spider" and the "cold,
calculated lie" of those who wilfully and maliciously
"misled" the masses by wild tirades and millennial
intimations. Even the saintly Gandhi was most cheaply
vilified as the "Dangerous Feminine Man". Similarly,

the trustees resented "the petty fanaticism of the meddlesome prigs", of their critics at home. The "calumny of the natives", as Bright called it, led in time to the slander of compatriots who refused to conform. The Baboos whom the sahibs abominated did not realize that the sahibs were not loved everywhere in England. The doctrine of trusteeship was tragically perverted by a racialism that was not essential to it, together with a messianic element that was imported into it. There was a mandate towards the natives as well as a mandate of responsibility to the civilized world. Imperialism was regarded as a wider, grander concept than nationalism. Representative government had to be sacrificed to responsible government. On the other hand, the transitional element in the doctrine of trusteeship could also not be completely forgotten.

Mill had spoken of the need to facilitate the transition of the subject people to a higher state of improvement. When he was Lieutenant-Governor, Lyall wrote: "One thing is sure; the natives all discuss our rule as a transitory state." This was not welcome to the trustees. Earlier, Lord Lytton had written that "we have had to choose between prohibiting them *(i.e.,* the natives) and cheating them, and we have chosen the least straightforward course". Later on, he said of Lord Ripon's policy, "Does it not mean, nay, ought it not to be taken as meaning that we, the English Government in India, feel ourselves in a false position from which we wish to extricate ourselves as quickly as possible?" No one appreciated and accepted the logic of the theory of trusteeship as fully as Sir

Henry Cotton or Lionel Curtis early in this century.
Lytton had already pointed to the mistake of the earlier
trustees that they could "hold India securely by what
they call good government". Main had showed that the
trustees could not help the dissolving force that Western
civilization had brought on traditional Indian society;
they could not supply social cohesion. In the late twenties
J.A. Spender attacked the other assumption of the
trustees, that they could appeal to the peasants over the
heads of the politicians or even that they understood
their needs and grievances better than men like Gandhi.

Was the doctrine of trusteeship inherently erroneous
and not merely vulnerable? Was it merely a theory
trotted out to justify what Cobden called "a gigantic
system of outdoor relief for the aristocracy"? Was it a
species of cant, a kind of moral slang? Was Hobson's
charge   of   hypocrisy   against   "phrase-mongering"
imperialists a denial of the validity of the doctrine of
trusteeship in theory as well as in practice? Could it not be
argued that every trustee abused his powers and that the
entire theory was an ideal fiction? The fact remains that
we cannot dispense with ideal fictions or pleasing
emotions or moral slogans in politics. The doctrine of
trusteeship provided what proved to be in practice more
a private moral code than a generally accepted theory of
government. It is possible to doubt the wisdom of
imperial conquest and yet to accept the moral problem
faced by colonial rule as requiring some sort of practicable
solution. There was in Burke a Platonic idealism regarding
what governments as well as individuals could achieve.

The chief merit of the old feudal system was that "it made power gentle and obedience liberal". He also appealed to Roman political practice based on the belief in private honour as the great foundation of public trust so that private and public virtues were harmoniously combined rather than mutually destructive.

If the Burkean doctrine appeared later on to be a formula borrowed from the missionary by the politician to cover up the naked fact of domination, this was because of the sense of alienation, the absence of mutual sympathy between rulers and ruled against which the theory of trusteeship must gradually break down even while bringing inspiration to the finest spirits among the possessors of a monopoly of political power. If they could not regard themselves as the trustees of the interests and fortunes of many millions, they could at least gain acceptance by their everyday acts as just conciliators in local disputes between men of different sects and castes and social groups.

5

BENTHAMITE UTILITARIANISM

I t was perhaps the lofty remoteness of the doctrine of trusteeship that made the Benthamite doctrine of utilitarianism so convenient both as a form of justification and as a practical basis of imperial rule. It is indeed ironical that a rather provincial creed should have achieved world-wide influence. Cromer had argued that if good use was made of imperial power, the British need not fear that they would be overtaken by the Nemesis which attended Roman misrule. It could, in fact, be contended that if the Roman Empire spread Christianity, the British Empire disseminated the creed of Utilitarianism. It resulted in the *malaise religieux* in India even if it did not, as many expected, sweep away the panorama of classic Hindu 'paganism'. The utilitarian creed, in general, despite its wide sway, did not excite much enthusiasm except among the utilitarians themselves, who constituted a sort of Whig oligarchy, with a few men of outstanding competence and a large quantity of self-satisfied, mediocre imitators. They rejected all transcendental talk of natural law and cosmic purpose and became conscious of the immediate possibilities of political power.

They were chiefly the heirs of Humean scepticism,

Hobbesian realism and the 'Theological Utilitarianism' of Cumberland and Paley, but they were not aware of this lineage so much as the living leadership of Bentham, 'the father of English innovation', 'the great subversive'. He swept away Burke's own abstractions, denounced complication as "the nursery of fraud" and set himself up as a simplifier. His belief in single judges, his deprecation of juries, his eulogy of summary modes of procedure, his contempt for the doctrine of separation of powers, his enormous faith in the potentialities of executive power and his conception of legislation as a panacea were all characteristic of his thought. For security against breach of trust, the sole apt remedy was, in his view, not impotence but constant responsibility, "substantial, punitional and dislocational". His concern was with authority, not liberty, individual or national. He was strenuously opposed to the notion of natural rights, "nonsense upon stilts". A Declaration of Rights, which to Burke was the "Digest of Anarchy", was to Bentham an evil, "the *ne plus ultra* of metaphysics".

Despite the arguments he supplied the Radicals, he came to the view that the colonies could not be emancipated. They were possible laboratories for social and political experiment. Even at the end of his life he said that Mill would be the living executive and he would be the dead legislative of British India. Mill was able to exercise a more direct influence as he was, in the language of the Radicals, a "retainer from the other side", a "demagogue" at home and a despot abroad. In his evidence of 1832 before the Parliamentary

Committee, he put forth his notion of a Government of India, supreme over all courts and persons, with absolute authority equal to that of the British Parliament and with a single legislative council of experts. It did not matter so much *who* governed as long as the business of government was discharged efficiently and cheaply. If the people were properly protected, their character would be elevated effortlessly. His son, J.S. Mill, also held a lofty view of the need for active supervision and control from London, as there was no practical alternative to a pure and enlightened, benevolent despotism. But he never denied the abstract right of India to self-governing institutions, and in this sense alone it could be said that he civilized utilitarianism.

Two years after Bentinck became Governor-General, Bentham wrote to Bentinck that he felt "as if the golden age of British India were lying before me". Bentinck declared that the first and primary object of his heart was the benefit of the Hindus and that a new morality and a new conception of the will of God would be useful in improving their future condition. "I write and feel as a legislator for the Hindus, and as I believe many enlightened Hindus think and feel." The same "enlightened principles" could promote in India as in England the general prosperity and also exalt the character of the British. They could, in other words, serve the material and moral interests of both nations; what better tribute could be paid to the unique usefulness of the utilitarian doctrine? Munro also held that the benefits of just laws and of moderate taxation were not enough unless an endeavour was made to raise the character of the natives.

Elphinstone, like Munro, pleaded for a policy of gradualness in encroaching on the institutions of India. They were proposing a *via media* between Burkean conservatism and Benthamite radicalism, but they were closer in spirit to the former and in their programme to the latter. Elphinstone had great respect for Bentham but would not consider himself a Benthamite and wrote to Malcolm about how difficult it was to reconcile "Maratha Mamool with Jeremy Bentham". He also said of Babington, the President of the Regulation Committee, that "if he exceeds in any way, he does so in Benthamising".

There was a large, forward-looking conception of what they were trying to achieve among the utilitarians in India. Macaulay spoke with feeling about the pacific triumphs of reason over barbarism in the "imperishable empire of our arts and our morals, our literature and our laws". Western, especially English, education was the great panacea for the regeneration of India. Further, but for the abolition of *sati,* Bentinck felt that he would be guilty of little less than "multiplied murder". Utilitarianism was not merely responsible for many reforms and material benefits by the middle of the nineteenth century; it introduced something more subtle and lasting. It spread a spirit of scepticism and curiosity, a willingness to judge every institution in terms of human reason and happiness, a spirit of innovation and social reform that required the initiative of the state for its fruition in a stagnant and decadent society, crippled by corrupt, pseudo-religious practices.

It could even be argued that if the British ruling class needed the influence of Burke more than that of Bentham, the conquered Indian peoples needed the ideas of Bentham more than those of Burke, which were to some extent part of Indian tradition and thought. Unfortunately, the utilitarians were carried away by their conviction that they were replacing the iniquities of 'oriental despotism' in an inferior civilization by the benefits of benevolent despotism that came from a more enlightened nation. It was not so much a policy of continued interference that was adumbrated. It was an attitude of mind, a tone of voice that was so lacking in the sceptical spirit of utilitarianism except when directed at the beliefs and institutions of others.

The culprit was chiefly James Mill and his weapon his highly overrated *History of British India,* but his complacency and insensitivity were common to the pundits if not the practitioners of utilitarianism. Mill singled out the Indians and the Chinese as particularly poor specimens of "uncultivated society", a far cry from the panegyrics they received in the eighteenth century from the thinkers of the Enlightenment. Hindu society, especially, was declared to be in such a hideous state that it was much inferior to Europe even in its darkest feudal age. And yet the utilitarians believed in the simple uniformity of human nature everywhere. This distorted and monotonously black picture of oriental civilization that the utilitarians had became the basis of even more extreme claims by men like Balfour early in this century.

Balfour declared that these great nations had got under the absolute government of the British "a far better government than in the whole history of the world they ever had before, and which not only is a benefit to them, but is undoubtedly a benefit to the whole of the civilized West". What was more, Balfour said in his Sidgwick Memorial Lecture* to Newnham that oriental nations could never escape from their primeval despotism. "We may crystallize and re-crystallize a soluble salt as often as we please, the new crystals will always resemble the old ones." Even the "obscure disharmony between the Imperial system and the temperament of the West" was blamed on the East. The Imperial system "was perhaps too oriental for the occident, and it certainly became more oriental as time went on". Even Western decadence resultant upon Western imperialism could be blamed on oriental despotism.

The utilitarians were preaching and practising in a climate of progress rather than of decadence; they had no serious qualms about being more authoritarian abroad than at home. They had not only taken social utility rather than tradition as the main criterion of social institutions and values. They also subscribed to a form

* *Decadence*, 1908, pp. 35-41.

of social determinism, to the results of forces that men are bound to accept one day. Hence their political messianism, maintained by the convenient belief in an identity of interests between rulers and ruled. Determinism was combined with a form of historicism and messianism was enriched by an element of utopianism. It was the task of legislators to identify the interests of various groups, to reconcile them and thus reveal their inner identity. Good laws could make virtuous men.

The rationalism that is implicit in utilitarianism was, of course, moderated by English empiricism and realism. The utilitarians made the exercise of absolute power subject to self-imposed rules, so that it ceased to be arbitrary and became dependable. A bridge was thus provided between the power-impulse of colonial administrators and Burke's exacting notion of moral responsibility. As Mill saw clearly, it was tempting to exercise vast power without commensurate responsibility in imperial territories; this was where utilitarianism came in handy. It was fortunate that the utilitarians in India did not sacrifice justice to utility or make utility so supreme that it displaced any independent notion of the good. If they did not generally bother about democracy or liberty, they were not alone in this respect. The doctrines of trusteeship and of utilitarianism had alike little use for representative institutions. Apart from this, the utilitarians were absurd rather than dangerous. Trustees could be solemn and utilitarians could be pompous. An extreme example was Macaulay, of whom Trevelyan wrote: "His topics, even in courtship, are steam navigation, the education of the natives, the equalization of the sugar duties, the substitution of the Roman for the Arabic alphabet in the oriental languages."

The utilitarians had their serious critics. Even the mid-century Radicals felt that the standard of utility was an intellectual concept too remote from the sentiment of the mass of people, whose relatives were toiling in oversea territories. At the same time utilitarians have been criticized for not going far enough, for not embarking on a more ambitious programme of social reform and of public works. Further, they have been attacked for their political materialism, for taking too narrow a view of happiness and being far more concerned with impersonal procedures and institutions than with the desires and dreams of men. Disraeli castigated what he called the "fallacy of supposing that theories produce circumstances" and of assuming that political institutions could be formed on abstract principles. The most reasoned criticism of utilitarian errors came from Maine on the basis of his sympathetic study of Indian society. He saw the injustice of James Mill's treatment of Indian history and life and deprecated the tendencies towards imposed uniformity and centralization in a land of time-honoured usages and diverse local customs and declining village communities. The modern idea of legislation was alien to a society which denied law-making authority to its rulers, who were required to leave established social practices undisturbed. A blind adherence to abstract symmetry would only lead to practical confusion.

Maine may have gone too far in his criticisms, but certain doubts and questions remain. Can an imperial authority exercised remotely through alien officials be properly aware of the wants, needs and the interests of the people? Can it ever take measures to promote the welfare of its distant subjects even at some sacrifice to domestic interests? How can imperial subjects be certain that references to the general interest of the Empire do not really mean only the interest of the ruling country? How to distinguish and decide between ephemeral interests and enduring sentiments or between current sentiments and long-term interests? These questions arise because an empire could never achieve in practice, perhaps not even in theory, the organic unity and the degree of social cohesion that might exist within a nation. These questions are easier asked than answered, but as to the continuing influence in India of the social reforms and the judicial and administrative and economic system that the utilitarians initiated there can be no doubt. The deeper consequence may well be their habit of endowing the rule of law with almost transcendental sanction, of securing for reason and utility the force of emotion and custom, of accepting rather than deploring the fact of political power and, above all, of showing that social change as well as stability is needed for happiness and social survival.

Whereas Burkean pragmatism was combined with a sure, firm sense of obligation, Benthamite utilitarianism, with its belief that political questions could only be treated by Baconian methods, was concerned with what was highly desirable rather than what was obligatory. Even in matters involving religious and moral principle, the utilitarians felt the need to consider consequences, balance probabilities, estimate forces and to choose the lesser evil. They were concerned in the sphere of politics with what was likely to do good or harm, not with what was definitely right or wrong, regardless of consequences. Whilst the trustee took pride in his intentions and his sense of responsibility, the utilitarian relied on results and his sense of achievement. In Hindu terminology, the former stressed *dharma* (duty), the latter emphasized *artha* (interest). Both of these had been neglected in India owing to an obsession with *moksha* (salvation), but the utilitarian doctrine was a greater blow to inertia than the doctrine of trusteeship was a shock to complacency. Indifference to the utilitarians was wholly impossible.

6

PLATONIC GUARDIANS

It was Seeley who first saw most clearly that the British were not able to astonish the Hindu as easily as they thought. They simply must find an idea with the power to move men and to show that the British conquest was moral rather than material, representing the triumph of the modern over the medieval and the ancient world. Neither dutiful piety nor daring philanthropy could buttress the self-confidence of the rulers or bamboozle the ruled with their hoary culture as much as the heroic mission of spreading the light of the New Learning and the Liberal gospel of progress. It was Jowett who showed how the Platonic doctrine of guardianship could be applied to India. In the fifties Philip Woodruffe elaborately used the Platonic model in his deeply felt, almost elegiac, apologia for the men who ruled India over the entire period of British domination. His book was profusely praised for not being like the "guilt-obsessed books" that distressed the reviewer in the *Sunday Times*.

In the *Republic* Socrates assures Thrasymachus that "there is no one in any rule who, in so far as he is a ruler, considers or enjoins what is for his own interest, but always what is for the interest for his subject or suitable to his art; to that he looks, and that alone he considers in everything he says and does". A careful selection must be made of those "who are the best guardians of their own conviction that what they think the interest of the state is to be the rule of their lives". It is necessary to safeguard against the watch-dogs turning upon the sheep and worrying them, behaving not like dogs but wolves; this was the task of the shepherds. They must receive such education as will have "the greatest tendency to civilize and humanize them in their relations to one another, and to those who are under their protection". They should not acquire so much property or wealth that they become housekeepers and husbandmen instead of guardians, enemies and tyrants instead of allies of the other citizens; "hating and being hated, plotting and being plotted against, they will pass their whole life in much greater terror of internal than of external enemies, and the hour of ruin, both to themselves and to the rest of the state, will be at hand". The guardians must be the smallest but the wisest of all classes in the state. The various classes should be kept from meddling with one another's occupations, as justice requires that no man is to have what is not his own.

Injustice arises with the production of a state of things at variance with the natural order. Where there is no common but only private feeling a state is disorganized – when you have one half of the world triumphing and the other plunged in grief at the same events happening to the city or the citizens. In an ideal state the guardians are regarded as saviours and helpers by the people, whilst the rulers call the people their maintainers and foster-fathers. The entire state constitutes a single family. The ideal can never be perfectly realized, and at least there must be philosopher-kings who combine political greatness and wisdom, and who do not pander to popular whims. Governments vary as the dispositions of men vary, for states are made, not of oak and rock, but out of the human natures which are in them; the states are as the men are.

This, in essence, is the much-abused Platonic model which is attractive in terms of its own assumptions, and which Woodruffe regards as "an ideal for the Indian system, not consciously adopted and exactly followed, for that is not the way English minds work". The English guardians were a small ruling class, an alien race, disinterested and aloof, "free from Platonic rigidity", with a real warmth for the Indian peasant, more concerned with peace and unity than with freedom, and by and large incorruptible. Their self-confidence was tempered by eccentricity, and such arrogance as they showed made them independent-minded. The despotic power they wielded was made bearable by the principle of delegation of authority coupled with full acceptance of personal responsibility. It was a despotism all the same, "as any system must be in which people are given what is good for them instead of what they want". These "amateur despots" were "expert in nothing or everything, answerable in practice mainly to themselves".

The English guardians were confident that the Indian Brahmins of the nineteenth century were not at all like Plato's guardians and soon became convinced that they themselves were, for all their foibles such as pigsticking! Each generation was, according to Trevelyan, more simple, more hardy and more pious than the last. As they grew older, these guardians were not as uniform, sedate and forbidding as Plato's but were distinguished, according to Woodruffe, for "their diversity, their humanity, and their oddness". Thus the English guardians gave India a system that Englishmen would never have tolerated for themselves.

Even if we accept Woodruffe's version of the Platonic model and his arguments to support the analogy, its implications for India must not be ignored. The advantages of the model were not only propagandist but also practical. It made a virtue out of the Prussian vice of self-glorification. It helped the ruling class and the ruling race to believe in its mission and its destiny. It facilitated the education and the discipline of the civil service and rendered its members capable of cultivating their own gardens as well as those of others. It provided an impetus to public justice and to private integrity. It weakened potential opposition to the regime, at least partially and temporarily. Above all, it prevented open oppression and fostered minimum standards of fairness within the framework of a system that took despotic power and prestige for granted. It made it impossible for national pride to be subordinated to trading profits or for grand opportunities and exalted moral conceptions to be sacrificed to "the pure bread-and-butter doctrines of the political economists". Even the radicals like Bright were happier to be guardians than to be trustees or utilitarians.

Thanks to the guardians, Western education and culture were brought to India through a state directive rather than private initiative. If the guardians were aloof, so were their willing and unwilling wards alike; if they became an exclusive caste, they could claim to be following the example of the Hindus, including those who were eager for Western education. Apart from anything else, they did not mind – in fact almost took pride in – being disliked. The resentment of the Indians could, after all, be put down to a sense of inferiority and the antipathy of other nations could be attributed, as Professor Cramb* argued in 1900, to *phthonos,* Immortal Envy. The Platonic model was naturally sustained by the comforting belief that the British guardians were irreplaceable, as a class, by Indians. To put this on a permanent footing required the importation of a racial element into the Platonic model. Instinctive race prejudice had to be made doctrinal. Every native was regarded as incorrigibly corrupt or inherently inefficient or both. Lord Northbrook complained to Lord Dufferin that the civil service has strongly imagined that "no one but an Englishman can do anything". Sir John Strachey went so far as to claim hereditary virtues, mental powers and physical courage

* *The Origins and Destiny of Imperial Britain.*

for the English, "those qualities necessary for the government of men, and which have given us an empire". The British guardians must always remain guardians because they alone possessed qualities that were proved by the fact that they were guardians, in the first place. These qualities unhappily did not render them safe from the absurdities of circular reasoning.

J.A. Spender summed up fairly the attitude of the guardians. "The old-style Indian Civil Servant was an ideal guardian for an Indian Peter Pan. He brought with him the public school and Oxford and Cambridge tradition with all the excellent things that go with it — chivalry, courage, fair-play, self-confidence, the sense of responsibility, the habit of command and complete integrity. . . . Within the limits that he set to them his services were beyond praise, and India would be basely ungrateful if she forgot them. But he conceived himself as presiding over an eternal nursery which would never question his authority and always require the same services to be performed for it. He fought for this theory very gamely. . . . But in the end he was his own undoing. . . the idea of governing a vast country of immense potential resources with a handful of public-school and university-trained men from another continent was bound to pass as soon as its people became conscious of their needs and had voices to express them."* When this happened, they complained that the policy of Indianization, like the grant of all political privileges,

* *The Changing East*, 1926, pp. 154-155.

was looked upon by their rulers as a reward for good conduct rather than as a training in political character.

All these elements in the Platonic theory of guardianship as applied to India found expression, at least embryonically, in Jowett's letters. He wrote to Lansdowne in 1888 that "there is more opportunity of doing great and permanent good in India than in any department of administration in England, and the office having more power is also more free from the disagreeables of home politics". Old civil servants deplored to Jowett that crowds and congresses are so unmanageable. "India for the Hindoo" was like "Ireland for the Irish" and universal suffrage in England would not allow them to be coerced. Jowett felt that native character was "so different from the European that we hardly understand it". He regretted that "in India as in England we are apt to do things rather too late — so in Ireland". Jowett saw the difficulty of reconciling "the hopes of the natives and the suspicions of the English" but he felt that universal kindness and attention was the best basis of popularity. He did not believe that the congresses were really dangerous, as educated men who were not more than 1/10,000 were not really to be feared even if they secured English Liberal support and even if they were the most active and energetic of men. He suggested that a great deal could be done by securing the allegiance of the princes, by conferring benefits on the masses and admitting them to a "somewhat larger share of administration". But he warned that "whenever we admit them to Representation they will flood and drown us".

He did not wish to deny that "the first duty
of the English rulers of India is to maintain themselves",
but couldn't the natives be conciliated without offending
the civil service? He felt that "the English and native
tempers can never harmonize. The Englishman has
no sympathy with other nations. He cannot govern
without asserting his superiority. He has always a latent
consciousness of the difference of colour." Was this a
recognition that the theory of guardianship could not
apply to the alien English in India? He had anyway
a feeling that "a good-humoured ignoring" of the
congresses was probably the right policy. "They should
be treated with the greatest courtesy and even
compliment, but of course, if they go beyond their
tether, they have to be stopped." He was convinced that
the precedents of the French Revolution or of the
English Reform Bill were out of place in India, although
to refuse any degree of representation was the height of
inconsistency and also it was impossible to govern India
without "a much larger infusion of the best natives".

The British, felt Jowett, should not be regarded as
conquerors. They must create a common feeling between
rulers and ruled for the good of India. There was a
native wisdom beyond the traditions of the civil service
and this must be tapped. When Jowett heard that there
was trouble in India in 1891, he wrote that it was well
not to lose time, for things move slowly. The phases of
politics were, in his view, like the changes of weather

and were always being forgotten. In 1892 he contended
that the difficulty of India was social rather than political,
as in England. As to the political question, he had
asserted ten years earlier that it seemed to him that the
Eastern must always be dependent on Western powers,
"on England above all". Within a century, even Indian
character might be visibly changed by education and
mainly by material causes. There ought to be a good
deal of Western supervision of Eastern officials, the one
supplying honesty and justice, the other knowledge of
the natives and aptitude for dealing with men. It was a
pity that the best boys from the public schools were not
being attracted in adequate numbers to the Indian Civil
Service.

On the whole, Jowett's political outlook is well
brought out in a letter he wrote in 1892 on the condition
of Russia, which seemed to be very miserable. "Do you
see any way of gradual improvement? Or are there
impossibilities in the nature of things? To grant strict
justice and toleration, not to Nihilists but to the Russian
people in general, seems not an impossible thing even
under a despotism. Cannot the Emperor be turned into
what Plato calls a virtuous tyrant? . . . I believe that the
Ambassador of a foreign nation may sometimes do for a
people what they cannot do for themselves, because he
sees the situation more clearly and he is trusted by the
monarch when his own ministers are not — only as in so
many other good things which have to be done he must
not be found out doing them — or at any rate as in all
difficult enterprises he must conciliate everybody and

everything."

The real difficulty with the Platonic model was that it could be easily perverted by the Aristotelian notion that some men are born slaves and that the laws of freemen could never apply to them. The doctrine of guardianship had its charms for imperialists like Milner, who was much excited over the task of maintaining the *pax Britannica* among a fifth of the human race. It was not by what it took away but by what it gave that imperialism sought to win subject races to itself. Further, as Churchill said in 1926, "Once we lose confidence in our mission in the East . . . then our presence in those countries will be stripped of every moral sanction, and cannot long endure." But the fact remained that there could be no common will or purpose between an alien race and the ruled, and hence, as Plato believed, the state was bound to disintegrate.

Guardianship was a grand ideal although unacceptable to a mature civilization, but no guardian could serve two masters or fulfil equally his two duties, to India and to England. Men like Gladstone were worried that England should take it on herself to act as the lawgiver, as foreigners were repelled by "too great a tendency to self-esteem — too little disposition to regard the feelings, the habits, and the ideas of others". The Platonic doctrine, however noble, could be corrupted by the Semitic notion of a chosen race as well as by a species of political Darwinism. Just as the revelations of Sinai and the promises of Jehovah did not concern the

Gentile, the Gospel of 1688 could not be revealed except to Englishmen. The expansion of England and the extent of the Empire showed the survival of the fittest.

There were, of course, those who would not accept the doctrine of guardianship. When Frere became Member of the Viceroy's Council, he expressed his dislike of "a policy which puts all real power into the hands of European officials and European colonists and treats the natives as at best *in statu pupillari*, to be ruled, taught and perhaps petted, but to be excluded from all real power or influence . . . and to be governed . . . according to our latest English notion of what is best for them". Even Salisbury, when he was Secretary of State for India, in 1875 put his finger on the central weakness of the doctrine of guardianship. In a speech to the students at Cooper's Hill College, he said that "no system of government can be permanently safe where there is a feeling of inferiority or of mortification affecting the relations between the governing and the governed. There is nothing I would more earnestly wish to impress upon all who leave this country for the purpose of governing India than that, if they choose to be so, they arc the only enemies England has to fear. They are the persons who can, if they will, deal a blow of the deadliest character at the future rule of England."* But, surely, was it not the height of unrealism to expect that this could be avoided when it was almost implicit in the

* Sir Henry Cotton, *The New India*, 1904 edn., p. 42.

theory and practice of guardianship and came to the fore when it was confronted with the bitter sense of alienation that wholly foreign rule produced?

Salisbury himself gained a brief notoriety in 1888 by his slighting reference to Dadabhai Naoroji's election as M.P. for Finsbury — "I doubt if we have yet got to that point of view where a British constituency would elect a black man" — for which the Prime Minister was severely castigated by Morley and Gladstone and apparently admonished even by the Queen. It is indeed asking too much to expect missionaries of civilization and self-appointed guardians to mortify their feelings of national pride and racial prejudice or even to moderate their collective sense of superiority. Trustees may neglect their responsibility and utilitarians may abuse their power, but it is even easier for the guardians of the State to fail to be guardians of themselves, as Plato required them to be.

7

EVANGELICALISM

urkean trusteeship, Platonic guardianship, even Benthamite utilitarianism could all become full-blooded theories that could justify and even sanctify British rule in India if a providential element could be imported into them. They could receive a supernatural sanction even if they were unable to secure popular acceptance or practical vindication or the gratitude of the natives. If the trustees could not be made accountable to a higher court of appeal on earth, they must at least be aware that they were answerable to God who had called them to their privileged position. The utilitarians, with all their worldly pretensions and their tendency to underrate human fallibility and sinfulness, could still be praised for their good works, which could be regarded as disguised acts of Christian charity. The utilitarian doctrine has even been described as a "side-wind from the main current of Christendom".

The guardians could be more effective if they could feel that they were divinely appointed to perform the sacred mission of civilizing the lesser breeds without the law or holy writ. If only the Hindus and the rest could be regarded as superstitious and unregenerate, ignorant of the divine word and the divine will and therefore specially prone to sin and error, vice and corruption, it would be so much simpler to explain the extravagances of 'oriental stagnation', 'oriental despotism' and 'oriental backwardness'.

It almost seems that if the evangelicalism of the Clapham sect, like the deity of Voltaire's universe, did not exist, it would have had to be invented. Fortunately, this was not necessary; evangelicalism flourished in its own right, even though it owed much of its impetus to the Indian connection. In fact, it existed before the other doctrines had been freely disseminated. Some have even assigned to Wilberforce rather than to Burke the credit for formulating the doctrine of trusteeship in regard to colonial possessions. This could be defended on the ground that by the abolition of slavery this great humanitarian rendered better services than Burke to the world as a whole. It is, in fact, indisputable that Burke formulated the doctrine of trusteeship more clearly and fully than anyone else, at any rate in England. But if Burke had greater influence on imperial administration, it was Wilberforce who really helped to create the British conscience in its attitude to colonialism. He once wished that the younger Pitt had resolved "to govern his country by *principle* rather than by influence".

Wilberforce has been described as "that rare migrant into public life", the man of principle who achieves important practical results while always being labelled in his own day as an idealist rather than a politician. Although he invoked the wrath of Cobbett and the satire of Hazlitt, he could never be written off as a crank in the patrician society in which he had moved by right of talents. He made evangelicalism eminently, almost painfully, respectable in its time. His strength was rooted in a religious faith which came to him with revivalist suddenness and made him a zealot rather than a prig.

The Evangelical Movement was the result of the influence of Methodism on the Church of England. It became the Low Church of Anglican Methodism just as the Wesleyan sect was the High Church of Nonconformity. Hence the superior respectability of evangelicalism. It was pietist rather than rationalist, propagandist rather than conservative. It consisted of a Cambridge group under Isaac Milner and Charles Simeon and of the Clapham sect, which included the Thorntons, Zachary Macaulay, Lord Teignmouth, formerly Governor-General of India, James Stephen and John Venn. Their Calvinism was of a mild variety, and Wilberforce was very impressed with the unscriptural character of the Calvinistic system. The evangelicals were men of action and emotion who abstained from theological subtleties or speculations. Theirs was a sentimental and a practical Calvinism. They could work with Protestants of every denomination, although they gradually persuaded themselves and others that they were the only true Christians.

They could be petty as in their sneers at Coleridge. It is perhaps not surprising that they could not take to a thinker who asserted that he who set up Christianity over truth would end up by exalting his own sect above all others and by finally loving only himself. The evangelicals were, however, shallow and narrow rather than selfish and narcissistic. Evangelicalism, as Halevy pointed out, "constituted a link, effected a transition between Anglicanism and Dissent, between the governing classes and the general public, as represented by the great middle classes". It transmitted the gospel of duty and the panacea of education, while stressing the sovereignty of individual conscience and the possibility of sudden illumination resulting in total transformation.

The evangelicals were certain that British dominion in India was a divine dispensation, almost a miracle. Charles Grant's treatise of 1792 on the state of society and morals of Asiatic subjects and Wilberforce's own speeches showed that the evangelicals, unlike Burke, were only too ready to draw up an indictment against a whole people. Grant felt that the people of India were lamentably degenerate and base, yet obstinate in their disregard of what they knew to be right. He was shrewd in envisaging an Indian counterpart of the European Reformation, but he was small-minded in his contempt of everything in India, religions and laws, arts and crafts, manners and habits, morals and even misery. The evangelicals inevitably judged religious beliefs and development by worldly success and power. The elevation of Indian character could go hand-in-hand with the extension of British commerce, for was not this arrangement providentially provided? A community of interest between rulers and ruled could be established if

India were Anglicized.

Wilberforce pleaded in Parliament that, owing to the "vast superiority even of European laws and institutions, and far more of British institutions, over those of Asia", the Indian community would only be too grateful to exchange "its dark and bloody superstitions for the genial influence of Christian light and truth" and to experience a substantial increase of civil order and security, of social pleasures and domestic comforts. The evangelicals had no doubts that they knew what was right and good for India as they knew what was right and good for England. They risked the imposition of English ideas on Indian soil because of their profound, almost touching faith that they were right. They took for granted that the heathen Hindoo in his darkness had to be enlightened by the English and meantime he had to be forced to abstain from what the light of gospel truth condemned.

The evangelicals, unlike some Englishmen of a later period, had no hesitations or reservations about the state of Western society or morality and really believed that they had nothing to learn from the East. They could not ever imagine a religious philosophy and mysticism that had nothing to do with the corrupt and repugnant social practices they saw or about which they heard gruesome stories. If they were sometimes prepared to consider a slower pace of reform and a less extreme form of interference, it was solely because they believed that undue haste would defeat its own ends and arouse

the suspicions and animosity of the natives. There may
have been differences of emphasis regarding tactics but
there was not any doubt about the long-term strategy of
the evangelical fanatics. They certainly could not
countenance the early policy of non-intervention in
religious matters of the East India Company.

Not only considerations of humanity or of moral
obligation but the very progress of the Christian gospel
and the success of the local missionaries required that
Indian society should be rapidly renovated. There was a
violent and desperate sense of urgency and little
gentleness and humility among these zealots who wished
to carry "the genial influence of Christian light and
truth". Sir John Shore, or Lord Teignmouth, was
prepared as Governor-General to connive at the activities
of the first Baptist missionaries in Bengal in spite of
their illegal entry into the country. This was not surprising
in view of his solemn sense of professional obligation.
"When I consider myself the Ruler of twenty-five millions
of people, . . . I tremble at the greatness of the charge. . . .
I consider every native of India, whatever his situation
may be, as having a claim upon me; and that I have not
a right to dedicate an hour to amusement further than
as it is conducive to health and so far to the despatch of
business." He looked forward to the time "when I must
render an account of my commissions as well as
omissions", not to Parliament but to God.

His successor, Wellesley, was less interested in
evangelical work but was happy to tolerate missionary

activities. Lord Minto had to implement a more cautious policy of religious non-intervention because of the Vellore mutiny but in time became increasingly liberal. His successors, Hastings and Amherst, felt they could not afford to risk disturbances, despite their personal regard for some missionaries. It was Bentinck's reforming policy that really fulfilled many of the intentions of the evangelicals.

Minto had complained against the "coarse and scurrilous invective against the most revered order of Hindu society", the threats of hell fire and damnation that had been bandied about in "the miserable stuff addressed to the Hindus" and confidently asserted that a just God will condemn no being without individual guilt. He was disturbed by missionary readiness to call out Atheism, Deism and persecution whenever a slip in their conduct had required to be rectified. Bentinck, on the other hand, was worried by Hindu rather than by missionary excesses. By abolishing an inhuman and impious rite such as *sati*, he felt that the Government would only be following, not preceding, the tide of public opinion. But he still remained aware of the dreadful consequences, in general, of a supposed violation of religious customs. At about the same time, Macaulay wrote to his father in 1836 that "if our plans are followed, there will not be a single idolator among the respectable classes of Bengal, thirty years hence". Yet a little over a decade earlier, Elphinstone had written, "To the mixture of religion . . . with our plans . . . I most strongly object." But Macaulay's attitude of optimism

was natural and consistent with the belief later on
expressed by John Lawrence thus: "We are here by our
moral superiority, by the force of circumstance, and by
the will of Providence . . . in doing the best we can for
the people we are bound by our conscience and not by
theirs."

The real problem raised by the evangelical and
messianic conception was not seen clearly until Lyall
wrote in 1872 that the Government had not only to
reconcile the interests and to recognize the peculiar
institutions of several powerful native creeds radically
distinct in structure and mutually hostile in temperament;
it had also to submit its proceedings to tribunals of
religious opinion in Europe as well as in Asia and "to
take account of theological prejudices in two continents.
So we are continually measured by inconsistent standards
and weighed in discordant balances." A regime that
prided itself on its individual and collective conscience
and set before itself a lofty role of trusteeship had to
contend with Hindu orthodoxy, Muslim iconoclasm,
the refined Deism of the Brahmo Samaj, Nonconformist
Radicalism and the accusations of expediency and
immorality levied by aggressive missionary societies.

Charles Kingsley defended the founders of the Brahmo
Samaj against the criticism of more orthodox Churchmen:
"I trust that no bigotry here will interfere with men
who, if they are not at the point to which St. Paul and
St. John attained, are trying honestly to reach that to
which Abraham, David, and the Jewish prophets rose: a

respectable height I should have thought." It was indeed
fortunate that the British began to govern India at a
time when religious excitement was at a low ebb at
home, and were thus able to avoid the terrible extremes
of fanaticism to which the Catholic nations of Europe
had already gone. And yet British toleration could never
mean a policy of perfect neutrality. If the Christian
minority could not formally secure a sheltered position,
if their opportunities for privileged access to the ears of
the government could not be wholly relied upon, at
least they could plead a policy of total disestablishment
and dissociation from all religious institutions. But this
only rendered the regime vulnerable to the Indian charge
that it was wholly without any acceptable sanction, that
it bore no relation whatever to the values held by the
common people, that it was a satanic despotism despite
its benevolent countenance, that it was an insupportable
system of *adharma.*

   The Mutiny of 1857 showed the Government's
dilemma; it was accused of treachery and deception
and an attempt to entrap them into Christianity
by those who rebelled; it was also regarded as
divine chastisement for denying and degrading their
own religion by missionaries and other fiercely puritanical
laymen, many of whom had "a bias towards such
combinations as the Bible and the sword". The British
were even regarded as following in the Moghul tradition of
pursuing and alternating between the incompatible
policies of tolerance and conversion, vainly "reconciling
the irreconcilable". Some evangelicals drew the

conclusion that no Hindu or Muslim holidays should be observed, that all recognition to caste must be refused and that the Bible must be taught in all schools. Frere, on the other hand, felt no need for compromise as there was really no contradiction. "There can be no safe rule of guidance for a Christian Government different from that of a Christian individual – to do as we would be done by." And what Colonel Edwardes and others would wish to do "is just what we would ourselves resist to the death if attempted on us, – not by Hindoos or Moslems but by a Roman Catholic or Greek autocrat".

Later on in the Victorian period this note of religious impartiality was obscured and the evangelical element in British rule assumed a new and vulgar form. Kipling helped to secularize evangelism or at any rate to generalize it to cover almost everything. As Gustave Hervé* has well shown, patriotism becomes a full-fledged religion in its own right. The country becomes a kind of divinity whose name it is impious to pronounce irreverently. The priests of the new religion are the professional soldiers. With this goes a crude contempt for the patriotism as for the religions of other people; there is a fierce hatred of heretics and infidels. Patriotic songs replace hymns, textbooks of history and civic education replace, or are combined with, the Bible and catechism, military costumes acquire the splendour of religious robes, religious 'mummeries' are replaced by military exercises and parades, the flag is saluted with the same fervour

* *My Country Right or Wrong.*

shown to religious icons and sacraments. And yet the moral code of men like Kipling was essentially chaste as well as brutal, heroic as well as childlike. It was the religious coating that offended men like Joynson-Hicks who protested: "I know that it is said at missionary meetings that we have conquered India to raise the level of the Indians. That is cant. We conquered India by the sword, and by the sword we shall hold it. We hold it as the finest outlet for British goods." But he exaggerated in his turn. The missionary spirit was "no mere sophism of unscrupulous imperialists" but a real emotion which would, of course, have horrified Warren Hastings.

The civilizing and Christianizing role of the imperialists easily acquired the mystic character of a crusade — "save that, instead of the Cross, its banner is the pale pink tegument of the dominant race". Cromer thought that colour prejudice dated from the world-discoveries of the fifteenth century, one of the results of which was "to convince the white Christian that he might, not only with profit, but with strict propriety, enslave the black heathen". There were eminent divines who thought that the people of hot countries might be enslaved. Nicholas V issued papal bulls applauding the trade in Negroes and hoped that it would end in their conversion. How did these notions enter into Protestant England of the late nineteenth century? They even led to acts that violated every religious canon, although ironically they were stimulated by an attitude of mind and a zeal that came originally from messianic, religious evangelism. Garratt courageously deplored "the long succession of murders and brutalities perpetrated by Englishmen upon Indians which either went unpunished or for which at the demand of the whole European community, only a small penalty was exacted". Sir Henry Cotton was also disturbed by the assaults on natives by Europeans that were of "frequent occurrence" and occasionally resulted in fatal consequences, whilst the trial of these cases "too often results in a failure of justice".

These incidents were aberrations but they were based on commonly held maxims, that "the life of one European is worth those of many Indians", that "the only thing that an oriental understands is fear", and that England had been forced to lose many lives and spend many millions to hold India, for which she merited more substantial recompense than "the privilege of governing India in a spirit of wisdom and unselfishness". Many English youths looked with contempt on the creatures, "half-gorilla, half-Negro", who appeared in Punch cartoons and regarded them as a "parcel of black heathen bodies and natives . . . worshipping sticks and stones, and swinging themselves upon bamboos like beasts". The noble humanitarianism of the early evangelicals thus tragically gave way to a vulgarized doctrine that caused much un-Christian brutality, no less evil than the un-Hindu cruelty of corrupt practices such as *sati.*

Today we see all this more clearly and impartially. It is significant that Lord Hemingford should pay a bicentenary tribute to Wilberforce in Westminster Abbey by asserting: "We have no excuse for complacency:

greed and injustice persist among all races; there are shadows and even stains on our record. But there are valid reasons for pride and thankfulness and many of them are directly or indirectly traceable to William Wilberforce, the great humanitarian, the father of the principle of trusteeship."*

Evangelicalism gave a sense of urgency, an intensity of zeal and a certain largeness of scope to British imperialism in India, lacking in the parish pump politics of little Englanders. It enabled imperialists to respond to the humanitarian impulse as well as to the missionary challenge, thus transmitting the humane spirit of the eighteenth century as well as the dour Puritanism and harsh Calvinism of earlier periods to England and its empire in the nineteenth century. It meant that a definite moral imperative and an ethical idea of imperial service were laid upon what otherwise might have been merely a mixture of commercialism and exploitation. Evangelicalism was elastic enough, for all its grim rigidity, to provide the basis for a campaign for the physical emancipation of slaves as well as for a crusade to justify the political enslavement of freemen. Its real weakness was that it assumed that "all the giving and serving, all the responsibility and all the sacrifice are on one side, and all the need, all the receiving, all the gratitude (if any) are on the other".

Further, the evangelical imperialists took risks that

* *The Times*, August 25, 1959.

they had perhaps no right to take, they did not see that "the axioms of Clapham were paradoxes in Calcutta", and they could not imagine that "a time comes when the divine mandate is exhausted, and then a change must be made, for the virtue has gone out of the work and both parties will suffer".* They were more successful in Anglicizing than in Christianizing India. Even the extent of effective Anglicization has been doubted. Sir Henry Lawrence wrote in 1932: "I used to hear of India being 'Anglicized'; but in my experience it was rather the other way. It was we who were being Indianized. I never met an Anglicized Indian. I saw and knew many who spoke and dressed like Englishmen; but they will never be English. They have too much to lose and to leave, and the ancestral mortmain grips them. It would be far easier for the detached Englishman to become Indian. For we went to India at a most plastic and impressionable age. . . ."†

The reasons for the failure of Christianization were seen by some administrators as well as missionaries. Cotton came to the view that as the Hindu mind naturally runs in a religious groove, its instinct is to recoil from any bold solution of its present moral difficulties which does not arise from the past religious history of the nation. At best, their attitude was but a compromise between Rationalism and Hinduism. Dr. Congreve tried to show why Christianity could not make any deep impression on the two powerful systems of 'Brahminism'

* William Paton, *The White Man's Burden,* 1939, p. 55.
† *Fifty Years,* 1882-1932, a Symposium, p. 164.

and 'Mahometanism'. "If in his contact with Brahminism the missionary puts forward the philosophical side of Christianity, the subtle mind of the Brahmin delights in the combat, and meets him with a counter-philosophy. There is matter for endless dispute, but there is no result. If more wisely advised, the missionary rests on the simple statements of Christianity, on the facts of its history and its appeal to the conscience of men, he spares himself personally the annoyance of defeat in argument, or the pain of seeing his arguments make no impression, but for his cause the effect is the same. For the religious system of India leaves its worshippers no sense of want. . . . The contest is not such as it was with the polytheistic systems of Greece and Rome. . . . On Mahometanism Christianity has made no impression, has tacitly renounced the attempt to make any. The rival Monotheisms met in the middle ages . . . Greek Christianity succumbed. Latin Christianity waged successfully a defensive war. . . . Each of the rivals claims for itself an exclusive possession of the religious belief of mankind. Both alike are rejected by the other. They rest side by side, convincing monuments of the exaggeration of their respective claims."*

Although evangelicalism failed to achieve its ends, it left its wider influence behind. Even if Christianity did not make many converts, its secularized expressions as well as the challenge of conversion itself stimulated and affected Indian thought and life. But the chief impact of

* Quoted by Sir Henry Cotton, *The New India*, p. 228.

evangelicalism was on the doctrines of Burkean trusteeship, Benthamite utilitarianism and Platonic guardianship. There were also other Christian elements besides evangelicalism, especially the notion of "penitence for the sins of our forefathers, with an anxious desire to expiate, if possible, their fault", but essentially a silent sense of duty and a profound conception of personal responsibility. But these other elements, however important, did not constitute a doctrine; they existed in spite of all the theories and reflected the influence of religion and morality on Victorian lives.

The evangelicals were able to modify as well as to affect the other doctrines. Their belief that legislation was powerless to change human character was an antidote against utilitarian legalism; their faith in Anglicization undermined the Burkean veneration for tradition and custom in India; their view of education as a universal panacea was opposed to the hierarchical notion of a Platonic élite. On the other hand, the evangelical zeal for reform, consciousness of destiny and sense of mission provided stimulation to the utilitarians, the trustees and the guardians, although at different times the evangelicals came closest to each of the others.

8

INTERACTIONS

The interaction between the four doctrines was too subtle and complex to be reduced to any simple scheme or stable relationship. There were affinities as well as contradictions between all of them, but collectively they had continuing force and even a strange unity that could not have come to the political theory of imperialism merely through any two, or even three of them. Although at different times different doctrines predominated even to the apparent exclusion of what were once rival theories, all the four elements were there in some form or the other, from the beginning to the end. It was natural that trusteeship should appeal especially to the British Parliament, utilitarianism to the imperial government in India, guardianship to the civil service and evangelicalism to non-official bodies and societies. More generally, Burke provided a moral code, Bentham a programme, Plato an attitude of mind, and Wilberforce a transcendental sanction and a belief in oneself. All these were somehow needed in the solemn business of ruling over a long period in a distant country and among a vast and alien people, thus combining philanthropy and profit, conscience and convenience, expediency and dogma, prejudice and pride. The feeling for principle had somehow to come to terms with the facts of power, whilst reason had to serve as well as to restrain emotion. It was not always easy, even in practice let alone in theory, to unite the four doctrines.

Benthamite utilitarianism stresses the idea of happiness as against the idea of duty, results rather than intentions, 'moral legislation' rather than 'moral pathology'. The word *utile*, the 'useful', has carried with it a double antithesis and been contrasted with the *honestum*, the 'worthy' or 'honourable', and the *dulce*, the 'agreeable' or the 'attractive'. Bentham himself felt that 'utility', which he borrowed from Hume, was an unfortunately chosen word as the idea it gives was "a vague one". The British imperialist could never consciously prefer the *utile* to the *honestum* even though he could often choose it against the *dulce*. The other three doctrines saw to this. Bentham himself recognized the "constant responsibility" of trustees as well as "the strictest and most absolute dependence" on their creators. He also appreciated the role of the guardians in relation to "the untaught and unlettered multitude", though he went too far for the imperialists in wanting the multitude "to occupy themselves without ceasing upon all questions of government (legislation and administration included) without exception. . . ." Of course, the Benthamite contempt for custom could never be reconciled with Burke's veneration, although Bentham could concede the occasional usefulness of custom.

Burke had reacted against the rationalism of the

philosophes and the nascent utilitarianism of Bentham. It is no less difficult to reconcile Burke with the conservative utilitarianism of Paley than with the radical utilitarianism of Bentham or what has been miscalled the revolutionary utilitarianism of Godwin. The moral state of mankind filled Burke with dismay and horrors. "The abyss of Hell itself seems to yawn before me." He felt that "nothing can be conceived more hard than the heart of a thorough-bred metaphysician. It comes nearer to the cold malignity of a wicked spirit than to the frailty and passion of a man. It is like that of the principle of evil himself, incorporeal, pure, unmixed, dephlegmated, defecated evil." This was, of course, directed against the abstractions and metaphysical presuppositions that he did not share or accept implicitly. But in this respect Burke was more typically British than Bentham and, therefore, more influential.

The British are nothing if not empirical as they take their own metaphysics of common sense for granted, but the British imperialist administration could not dispense with the need which the Prusso-German bureaucracy heartily welcomed, the need for "a metaphysical smoke screen". Benthamite utilitarianism was far more than this and entered into practical programmes even while the Burkean spirit was never lost. This was because the Burkean doctrine could appear too static a concept of empire, a majestic posture of masterly inactivity, and at different times the need was felt for a dynamic force, a new vitality in imperial rule. But the supreme merit and use of the Burkean doctrine, against all considerations of reason and utility, was that it provided the decisive argument in favour of the given system, as against all imaginable conceptions of a future which is no more than possible — that it *exists* and that it is the necessary consequence of the past. Further, Burke was famous whilst Bentham was still obscure; the prophet got in before the pamphleteer. The Burkean doctrine went so deep that it later on modified the Platonic one. The guardians were required to wield their power by delegating it while at the same time assuming full responsibility for everything because of their private conviction that each had made a pact with his country and with God.

Burke and Plato combined to set before the administration extremely high standards by which it was inevitably found to be wanting by Englishmen as well as by Indians. This is not so much a pointer to dishonesty and deceit as a proof of pride and high idealism, of spiritual ambition as well as an exalted ethic. The Burkean doctrine was easier to invoke than the Platonic was to justify the withholding of representative institutions which could train the wards and treat them as pupils in representative government. On the other hand, the Platonic doctrine was more easily perverted by the poison of race prejudice than the Burkean doctrine. The Platonic doctrine could be used to combat every notion of equality. The Burkean doctrine could show the awful conflict between the 'pseudo-liberalism' of granting representative government and the staid conservatism of permanently retaining trusteeship. Race prejudice came later than the opposition to representative institutions and reinforced it. Men like Mayo and Lawrence, Canning and Dalhousie, were against any distinction of class or race. Lawrence even appreciated the role of trustees in regard to self-governing institutions. In 1864 he said: "The people of India are quite capable of administering their own affairs; the municipal feeling is deeply rooted in them. The village communities, each of which is a little republic, are the most abiding of Indian institutions. Holding the position we do in India, every view of duty and policy should induce us to leave as much as possible of the business of the country to be done by the people." This view was naturally rare.

The four doctrines had been united by the view, chiefly spread by the evangelicals, that India was no good for anything, and seemed to enjoy tyranny. Even Macaulay had said that it would be as absurd to establish popular governments in certain countries as "to abolish all the restraints in a school or to untie all the strait-waistcoats in a madhouse". And yet later on the Burkean and Platonic doctrines could combine to enable imperialism to take credit even for the nationalism that it unwittingly created. In the twentieth century, the 'theory of decolonization' originally put forward by socialist imperialists like Ramsay MacDonald could be assimilated into the political theory of British imperialism in Asia. The four doctrines could be made to serve different purposes at different times. In the latter part of the nineteenth century they could be given a Hobbesian coating. Stephen had said that "earth resembles heaven in one respect at least. Its kingdom suffereth violence, and the violent take it by force." Austin was always worried that political or civil liberty had been erected into an idol by "doting and fanatical worshippers". Stephen and Austin were thinking of England and not only the Empire.

In 1886 Lord Dufferin, a year after the birth of the Indian National Congress with his consent, had reiterated the role of the government as "an isolated rock in the middle of a tempestuous sea, around whose base the breakers dash themselves simultaneously from all the four quarters of the heavens". This view was a constant theme throughout the duration of the British Empire in India. There was the idea that Indians respected power, that they could easily be intimidated by force. There was also the British pride in being disliked, a sense of achievement in indifference to popular demands. The four doctrines resulted in the supreme paradox that the imperial rulers, who could not put their trust in princes or in politicians, in the old feudal or the new professional classes, unintentionally helped to democratize India, while adhering to their own polite form of autocratic government. Only the aliens could give good government to a disunited country and only they could be compelled to grant self-government to a united nation. All four doctrines were held with utmost sincerity, which the cynics who claim superior honesty can deny only at the expense of truth. All four doctrines were abused as well as misinterpreted, whilst the apologists who claim superior knowledge can deny only at the expense of justice.

9

CHANGING POLICIES

It is important that we should not ignore that other elements existed besides these four doctrines or that British rule in India went through a baffling variety of phases. The four doctrines do not go to make up a symphony; there were too many discordant notes, too many jerks and surprises, too many disagreeable noises. If there was a symphony, it sounded at times as if it could have been by Beethoven and at other times as if it was by Bartok. In any case, it was a form of music to which few Indians could respond. Warren Hastings had enunciated the need to combine power with responsibility, the need for strong as well as good government, the need to rule according to Indian customs, the need to protect the customary rights of the ryots, the need for centralized and direct control over all British dominions in India.

He had urged in 1772 the necessity of experiment. "We must adopt a plan upon conjecture, try, execute, add, and deduct from it, till it is brought into a perfect shape." The next year he criticized not his predecessors but rather "the want of a principle of government adequate to its substance, and a coercive power to enforce it". In 1804 Wellesley felt that "the position in which we are now placed is suited to the character of the British nation, to the principles of our laws, to the spirit of our constitution, and to the liberal and comprehensive policy, which becomes the dignity of a great and powerful empire".

In the intervening period between Hastings and Wellesley there had been the attempt of Cornwallis to impose his Whig conception of English landed society and to create an Indian aristocracy. Teignmouth had come to the view that "if we should confer happiness upon them, it will be in spite of themselves". With his evangelical sympathies, he naturally felt: "Every hour I stay in this country, my situation becomes more irksome. . . . The knowledge, such as it is, which I have acquired of the people, their customs and manners, does not make me like them the better." Minto who followed Wellesley reaffirmed the declared principle to protect the followers of each religious system in "the undisturbed enjoyment of their respective opinions and usages; neither to interfere with them ourselves, nor to suffer them to be molested by others". It was important to establish a system of administration best calculated to promote the confidence and conciliate the feelings of the natives, not less by a respect for their own institutions, than by the endeavour gradually to engraft upon them such improvements as might communicate to every class of people, under the safeguard of equal laws, "that sense of protection and assurance of justice, which is the efficient spring of all public prosperity and happiness".

With Bentinck there came a determination to found "British Greatness upon Indian Happiness", to inaugurate the age of reform and to curb "barbarous excesses" by legislation as well as by education. Munro went further and hoped that "we shall in time so far improve the character of our Indian subjects as to enable them to govern and protect themselves". Elphinstone, on the other hand, was concerned that "we have dried up the fountains of native talent, and that from the nature of our conquest not only all encouragement to the advancement of knowledge is withdrawn, but even the actual learning of the nation is likely to be lost, and the productions of former genius to be forgotten". When we come to Dalhousie, "a Scotsman bred on the Shorter Catechism", we meet with the postulate that it was not only the right but the duty of the paramount power to lose no legal opportunity of suppressing dependent states and substituting its own direct rule, of suppressing native usages and practices where they seemed to be barbarous and establishing the entire apparatus of Western civilization.

The tragedy of the Mutiny came as a shock to the complacency of the rulers, and it was followed by the Queen's proclamation eschewing racial discrimination and religious intolerance and affirming the obligation to maintain "the ancient rights, usages and customs of India". In the sixties Lord Lawrence felt that "great public benefit is to be expected from the firm establishment of a system of municipal administration in India". Earlier, Frere had hoped that there would be a large and an increasing school of officials "who hold with Hastings and Cornwallis, Wellesley, Malcolm and Montstuart Elphinstone rather than with Lord Dalhousie and Mr. Thomason and the later school of levelling, resumption and annexation". In fact, British rule during the remaining period was more ambivalent than ever, with sharp contrasts between Lytton and Ripon, Dufferin and Curzon, Reading and Irwin. In England itself, there was the fierce antagonism between Gladstone and Disraeli. Gladstone talked of the imperial mission to shed the light of liberty on other lands, whilst Disraeli asserted plainly that self-governing colonies were a contradiction in terms and that the Empire was a proud and permanent possession that lent a living prestige to the British heritage. Others argued that Britain, as the country which understood liberty best, had a unique right to rule over other peoples and races. Cromer declared that it would probably never be possible to make a Western silk purse out of an Eastern sow's ear. Lyall could even plead that "Indian spirituality is against the ideas and institutions of self-government."

With Curzon came the plea that official and non-official Englishmen should stand together and not reproduce ever again the mutual animosity that came to a head with the Ilbert Bill under Ripon's viceroyalty. Addressing the mine-owners at Burrakur, he declared: "My work lies in administration, yours in exploitation." Mill's warnings that the English in India must be either administrators or exploiters were forgotten or spurned. After Curzon the spirit of liberalism asserted itself again, but Morley could write to Minto, "Not one whit more than you do I think it tenable or possible or even conceivable to adapt English political institutions to the nations who inhabit India." This 'hierophant of liberalism' suspected that what the political classes in India "really want a million times beyond political reforms is access to the higher administrative posts of all sorts". The demand for freedom was despised as a cloak for crude ambition. In 1910 Ramsay MacDonald asserted that "efficiency is not better than self-government". In 1920 he declared that "unless the British political genius is to change fundamentally for the worse, the British conquest is to issue in liberty and self-government". This had already been argued by the Round Table Group of Lionel Curtis, and Chelmsford came under this influence. He and Montagu felt that the desire for self-determination was the inevitable result of education in the history and thought of Europe.

Later on, the Report on Indian Constitutional Reform combined a theory of political liberalism with a doctrine of active state intervention. It declared that "English theories as to the appropriate limits of state activity are inapplicable in India and that if the resources of the country had to be developed the Government must take action." The wheel had come full circle. The triumphant utilitarianism of the exponents of a theory of enlightened despotism in the early decades of the nineteenth century now returned under the guise of a new conception of state socialism. This was used, together with the exigencies of war, the Burkean conception of trusteeship adapted to the interests of minorities, as well as the inability of the Platonic guardians to grow up and face the facts of life around them, to delay the consummation that had been envisaged by Munro, Elphinstone and even by Macaulay. In the end it had to come.

The evangelicalism of the past had gone and the doctrines of Burkean trusteeship, Benthamite utilitarianism and Platonic guardianship had lost their ancient flavour and authentic fervour. Anachronistic survivals like Lieut.-Colonel Wyllie* of the Indian Army and the India Defence League ranted in vain against "the dreamers, dogmatists and defeatists" among their own compatriots. The willingness of the English spirit prevailed over the weakness of its imperial flesh.

The diversities among the men who ruled India and the contradictions between the various doctrines that they invoked must not make us forget the nature of the system that was set up and eventually had to be abandoned. It was a centralized, enlightened despotism that was transformed in time into an elaborate, autocratic bureaucracy. The despotism was softened by a spirit of tolerance, the bureaucracy was tamed by a tradition of equity. The Government of India was described by Lytton as a "government by despatch-box tempered by an occasional loss of keys". Like every despotism, it was based on the principle that everything had to be done for the people as they could do nothing themselves.

* *India at the Parting of the Ways — Monarchy, Diarchy, or Anarchy?* 1934.

There was sometimes, as under Curzon's rule, a tension between personal autocracy and the collective bureaucracy.

As the system lacked any principle of justification that derived from the beliefs and values of the people over whom it ruled, it was often induced to support its policies by the simple plea of *raison d'état*. Apart from power-oriented notions of authority, the utility of non-material incentives to the men who administered the system was fully recognized and largely met; they had to, and were helped to, believe in themselves. Utilitarianism was implicit in the system and compensated for the highly inadequate degree of communication between the ruling élite and the various social classes in the country. The system required a class of interpreters, a class of persons "Indian in blood and colour but English in tastes, in opinions, morals and intellect", but these interpreters became either ineffective or inconvenient as a class. They either lost touch with their own people or were not content to go on being disloyal to them. The system created economic as well as social and cultural problems that it could not solve. Agrarian and industrial revolutions were begun but could not work themselves out fully or fruitfully under the conditions of imperial rule.

There were inevitable contradictions inherent in the system. There could not be any harmony of political aims or cultural ends between the rulers and the ruled. The centralized system had to be maintained

by a policy of 'divide and rule' even if some thought it
to be the only way of ensuring fairness to all social and
religious groups. It could not carry out its duties both to
the British nation and to the Indian people with equal
ease. It was naturally prone to inertia, to follow the
maxim of Mendoza, the first Viceroy of new Spain: "Do
little and do that slowly."* Hence Jowett's complaint
that it had become an English habit to do the right thing
in the wrong way, to do too little and to do it too late.
Every centralized bureaucracy is, in a sense, a failure,
but especially so if it is administered by an alien people.
Often, the wrong thing was done in the right way rather
than the other way about because what the system
lacked by its very nature was partly supplied by the
moral code and personal qualities of the men who ran
the system.

* R. Syme, *Colonial Élites,* 1958, p. 60.

10

THE NATIONALIST RESPONSE

I t is easy to see why Indian nationalists concentrated their attack on the system rather than on the men who administered it, especially after Gandhi came along to show that this was required by Indian religious ethics and tradition. Before him it was common to attack the men for their inability to carry out their own high standards, to take their political beliefs on their face value. But at different times the four main doctrines of British imperialism were challenged by Indian nationalists, quite apart from their attack on the system. In the early decades of the nineteenth century, Metcalfe had written, "All India is at all times looking out for our downfall." Bentham at the same time referred to Ram Mohan Roy as his "intensely admired and dearly beloved collaborator in the service of mankind".

Roy was very impressed by Bentham's notion of the duty of resisting the Government in case the benefit to be secured by this is greater than the evil of revolution. He said, "If mankind are brought into existence, and by nature formed to enjoy the comforts of society and the pleasure of an improved mind, they may be justified in opposing any system, religious, domestic or political, which is inimical to the happiness of society or calculated

to debase the human intellect." He also believed that
enemies to liberty and friends of despotism have never
been and never will be ultimately successful. Democracy
and imperialism were incompatible, but it was better to
rely on the enlightened public opinion of England than
to be governed by a bureaucratic legislature. Ranade, on
the other hand, who was born almost a decade after
Roy's death, combined a Burkean view of the State with
a Benthamite theory of social reform, and also had his
own belief in India as a chosen race and challenged the
British claim to be a superior caste of eternal guardians.
The State in its collective capacity "represents the power,
the wisdom, the mercy and charity of its best citizens".
He preached a philosophy of moderation and liberalism,
stressing the need for justice between man and man,
giving to the rulers the loyalty that is due to the law
they are bound to administer but securing at the same
time to the ruled the equality which is their right under
the law. He was prepared to accept foreign interference
in social matters on utilitarian grounds that were different
from those that had been used by the Benthamites like
Bentinck.

Ranade shrewdly argued that the foreign rulers
have no interest to move of their own accord. "If they
consulted their selfish interests only, they would rather
let us remain as we are, disorganized and demoralized,
stunted and deformed, with the curse of folly and
wickedness paralyzing all the healthy activities and vital
energies of our social body. The initiation is to be our
own, and based chiefly upon the example of our

venerated past, and dictated by the sense of the most representative and enlightened men in the community." He pleaded that the foreigners were merely giving the responsible sense of progressive Indian thinkers the force and sanction of law in matters such as *sati* and infanticide and the recognition of the validity of widow marriages.

Benthamite utilitarians were unwittingly serving the cause of Hindu tradition and the stability of Hindu society, which Burke respected, by their reforms. They helped to bring about a Hindu Renaissance and a Hindu Reformation rather than a total revolt against religious tradition, let alone a massive conversion to Christianity. As Ranade said, "the change is sought not as an innovation, but as a return and restoration to the days of our past history. Those who advocate it justify it on the authority of texts revered, and admitted to be binding to this day. The intermediate corruption and degradation was not of the nation's seeking. It was forced upon it by the predominance of barbarous influences, and by the intolerance of ruthless conquerors."

If men like Balfour could later on argue that Western decadence was caused by oriental despotism and imperialist ideas imported from the East, Ranade was convinced that Indian decadence, which no one could doubt, was caused by Moghul despotism and British imperialism. He, too, like the evangelicals in England, had his own notions of divine dispensation and Hindu pride. "It was not for nothing that God has showered His choicest blessings on this ancient land of Aryavarta. We can see His hand in history. Above all other countries we inherit a civilization and a religious and social polity which have been allowed to work their own free development on the big theatre of Time."

The liberal, utilitarian and Burkean elements in Ranade's thought were directly transmitted to Gokhale in Poona, whilst the exclusive and providential element was independently pushed to violently messianic extremes in Calcutta by men like Vivekananda and Aurobindo. Ranade's direct answer to Benthamite utilitarianism took the form of a special theory of Indian economics which was combined with a theory of imperialist exploitation – the 'Drain Theory' – of Dadabhai Naoroji, put forward long before Ranade wrote, in 1870.

All this represented a marked change since the thirties in Bengal, when Western doctrines were uncritically accepted and could not, therefore, be turned against British imperialism, despite the splendid example set by Roy, whom Ranade regarded as one of India's greatest men. Roy was a universalist in religious but not in secular matters and could not accept the Benthamite notion that there were universal principles that could be applied to legal codes everywhere. Of course, he cherished the Indo-British connection as a decisive step towards universal brotherhood. The young Bengali intellectuals of the thirties, however, were not only good loyalists but also blind imitators. "In matters of politics, they are all radicals and are followers of Benthamite principles", commented *The Englishman* in 1836. A critic of secular education like Tarachand got Benthamism upside down and pleaded for moral education "which recognizes, above all, the grand deontological maxim of Bentham, that a man's duty to do, cannot but be also his interest".

The period between Roy in Bengal and Ranade in Bombay, between the thirties and the nineties, saw many drastic changes of thought that were achieved through a confusing variety of phases. In 1858 Harishchandra Mukherjee, in an article in *The Hindu Patriot,* asserted that the time had nearly come when all Indian questions must be solved by Indians. The emergence of the educated middle class as a new force had upset the old equilibrium of the constitution between the civil service, the supreme court and the *zamindars,* the three estates of the Indian realm. Soon the influence of Montesquieu and Bentham gave way to that of Buckle and Mill. In 1873 Asutosh Mukherjee stoutly defended Mill against the attack of Fitzjames Stephen, and also criticized Austin's theory of sovereignty. "How long and how often is obedience to be rendered in order that it may be habitual?" he asked. Jogendranath Vidyabhushan, on the other hand, quoted Charvaka to prove the fraudulent character of the ancient Brahmins. He believed that the positivism of Comte was the coming religion of the world.

In 1883 Saurindramohan Tagore wrote a book, *Hindu*

Loyalty, quoting ancient Indian texts in support of loyalty to Queen Victoria. Nabagopal Mitra agreed with Mill that despotism was more suited to India at the time than representative government, but felt a monarchy was a lesser evil than an oligarchy of foreigners. Sisirkumar Ghosh, however, felt that India had become fit for a democracy and had passed the tribal and then the centralizing or despotic phase that every nation must pass through. Imperialism, he felt, was harmful not only to the conquered but also to the conqueror. It was really Bankimchandra who effectively tried to reinterpret Indian political ideas in the light of Western thought and to convert the political theory of British imperialism into the political theory of Indian nationalism. He found traces of Benthamite utilitarianism in the Indian epics and in the *Bhagavad Gita,* but he felt that it only accounted for a part of *dharma.* He was also influenced by Mill's individualism and Comte's *Religion of Humanity.*

He became directly concerned with the two essential elements in nationalism, the method of identification of the individual interest with the welfare of a particular community, and the method of differentiation of the interest of the particular community from other communities. Neither of these elements had been present in India, with its extreme individualism combined with an exacting universalism. He felt that the only way to achieve results was to exalt patriotism to the dignity of a religion by relating it to the love of humanity. His entire doctrine of nationalism was

taken over by Bepin Chandra Pal and Aurobindo
Ghosh, whose messianic fervour was more directly fed by
the message of Vivekananda, who passionately pleaded
that India, with its unique mission and destiny, must
once more conquer the world through its religious
philosophy and its spirituality. "There is no other
alternative, we must do it or die."

The methods of Indian nationalists, in their challenge
to the theory of British imperialism, were of marked
variety. There was the appeal to British qualities of
fair-play and justice, a method used by the early
'moderates' as well as by Naoroji, co-founder of the
Congress, who ended up as an 'extremist'. There was the
challenge to the imperialist doctrines on the basis of
other elements in Western political thought, the invoking
of Paine against Burke and natural rights against the
duties of trustees, of Mill against Bentham and
representative democracy against utilitarian despotism,
of Mazzini against Plato and national destiny against
imperial guardianship, equality under natural law against
the special claims of the evangelicals. There was the
attack on the system on theoretical as well as practical
grounds and on some of the men who represented its
inherent vulnerability. Finally, there was the Gandhian
challenge to British behaviour, theory and the system in
terms of Indian ethical standards, political and religious
conceptions, and national aspirations.

Burke had written that "a kind of Providence has
placed in our breasts a hatred of the unjust and cruel in

order that we may preserve ourselves from cruelty and
injustice". Naoroji echoed this sentiment when he said in
1869 that the Englishman is incapable of despotism. "He
might, and often did, carry things with a high hand, but
the instinct and love of liberty, the constitutionalism
which is born with and ingrained in him, made him at the
time of trial recoil from being stigmatized a despot."
Indians should have a parliament in India as their goal,
but meantime the educated had to play the role of
Platonic guardians and educate the people to prepare
them for representative institutions. In 1882 Naoroji
was deeply rooted in his 'Drain Theory' but wrote to
Hyndman about his hope of results if the English
labouring classes could be moved, and about the
need for "educating England in the great Indian
question". He was despondent because "the Liberals
seem to be eating their own words. The feeling of
despair comes over me sometimes, but perseverance is
absolutely necessary. For efforts in a right cause
the result sometimes comes when least expected." If
the present material and moral destruction of India
continued, however, a great convulsion must inevitably
arise, unless an English statesman arose to do "what the
world should expect from English conscience, and from
England's mission to humanity".

Naoroji soon became pained by the contradiction
between English constitutionalism at home and liberalism
in Europe, on the one hand, and her "despoiling
despotism in India under a pseudo-constitutionalism",
on the other. The English were descending to "the lower

level of Asiatic despotism", a concept that Naoroji
borrowed from English writers. In 1897 Naoroji, a deeply
disillusioned man, roundly declared that "the unrighteous
and un-British system of government" was responsible
for "an unceasing and ever-increasing bleeding" of India
and was "maintained by a political hypocrisy and
continuous subterfuges, unworthy of the British honour
and name, and entirely in opposition to the wishes of
the British people". Disaster to the Empire would be the
inevitable result. This was a recurring theme in Congress
Presidential Addresses.

At this time many Indian nationalists were convinced
that the era of mendicancy, of petitions and moral
appeals, was finally to be ended. Just as imperialists
believed that the Oriental only respects power, so many
nationalists now declared that the Occidental and
particularly the hypocritical and moralizing British
could only understand the language of force and the
concreteness of organized violence. This meant the force
of words as well as of arms. There was no more question
of claiming freedom. "Swaraj is our birthright", declared
Tilak. Paine's powerful attack on Burke was widely read
and deeply absorbed. Man had no property in man, the
authority of the dead could not be invoked against the
rights and the freedom of the living. No nation had a
divine right to rule over another. A revolt was proper
against "the despotism of principles" rather than of
men. The imperialists venerated power and not principles.
There was no "monopoly-government of wisdom" of
wiser men of Gotham, of Platonic guardians. The masses

could not be looked upon as a herd of beings that must
be governed by fraud, effigy and show. The principle of
trusteeship was false because it presumed to renounce
the rights of all posterity in the name of fictitious
obligations to dubious ancestors.

In 1930 the Congress adopted a resolution in favour
of Purna Swaraj, or complete independence, which spoke
the language of Paine with the detachment and calm
dignity of Gandhi. Gandhi inherited the tradition of
Gokhale, whom he regarded as his guru, as well as that
of Tilak. At a time when the 'extremists' were inclined
to use the arguments of Paine in conjunction with the
wholly different principle that the end justifies the means,
that flavoured of the notorious English pamphlet of
1657 by Colonel Sexby *(Killing No Murder)*, Gokhale,
the greatest of the 'moderates', spoke with the political
outlook of Burke and the moral fervour of Bright. He
appreciated the temporary role of Platonic guardians
but firmly rejected the principle of State landlordism.
He appealed to the trustees to do their duty under a
sense of self-restraint as they did not yet have to contend
with the power of the electors as in England.

In 1902 he urged the need for a Government, national
in spirit though foreign in personnel. He contrasted the
narrower imperialism based upon race superiority with
"that nobler Imperialism which would enable all who are
included in the Empire to share equally in its blessings and
honours". But Gokhale, like Naoroji had done earlier,
stiffened in his attitude during the viceroyalty of Curzon

and what was called "the Russianization of the Indian Administration". Without sympathetic imagination no man could ever understand an alien people. Gokhale cited Gladstone's dictum, "it is liberty alone which fits men for liberty", against the counter-doctrine, "wait till they are fit". He compared Curzon with Aurangzeb whilst others had produced the false parallel of Akbar. With Curzon as with Aurangzeb, "we find the same attempt at a rule excessively centralized and intensely personal, the same strenuous purpose, the same overpowering consciousness of duty, the same marvellous capacity for work, the same sense of loneliness, the same persistence in a policy of distrust and repression, resulting in bitter exasperation all round". And yet the Indian 'extremists' hated Gokhale more than they hated even the British, just as the Mazzinians hated Cavour more even than they hated the Austrians.

In 1908 Aurobindo Ghosh had argued that the reason why even "a radical opportunist like Morley" refused Indians self-government was not that he did not believe in India's fitness for it but that he did not believe in India's determination to be free. Aurobindo attacked the "brief magic abracadabra of despotism", the semantics of imperialist self-justification which turned the peaceful acts of patriots into the illegitimate activities of criminals. He eschewed abstractions and formulas and spoke of practical necessities, the teaching of political experience, common sense and the world's history. Further, he said, "We recognize no political object of worship except the divinity in our Motherland, no present object of political endeavour except liberty, and no method or action as politically good or evil except as it truly helps or hinders our progress towards national emancipation." His attitude to bureaucratic concession was that of Laocoon: "We fear the Greeks even when they bring us gifts." In 1902, B.C. Pal spoke the language of Mazzini. India had its own special mission and its own peculiar destiny in the midst of humanity. "We desire to be in our own country as other peoples are in their country. We claim the right of controlling the course of historic evolution ourselves. We desire our own good and our own place in the universal scheme of things, and bear no ill-will towards any other people or country."

Lala Lajpat Rai challenged the basis and sanction of the law under imperialist rule. "Only one feels disposed to smile when one hears of Indian nationalists being charged in British-Indian courts with attempting to subvert the government established by law. One is inclined to ask 'By what law?' and 'Who made that law?' " Rai felt that so long as there were Curzons, Macdonnels and Sydenhams in the English Parliament, Indian nationalism would not starve for want of congenial food. If British imperialists could sometimes be aroused to a sense of guilt, at least all patriots had to be aroused to a sense of shame at the affronts to their dignity and their cultural and political identity.

Among nationalists it was commoner to attack the

imperialist system than to appeal to an individual sense of guilt. Gokhale declared: "It is the system which is really at fault — a system which relegates the interest of the people to a very subordinate place, and which, by putting too much power into the hands of these men, impairs their sense of responsibility and develops in them a spirit of intolerance of criticism." Surendranath Banerjea had said this as early as the seventh Congress: "It is not the men who are to blame; it is the system; it is the bureaucracy, the absolute despotism, that has been established, that must be arraigned before the bar of public opinion in India and throughout the civilized world." At the twenty-ninth Congress in 1914, Bhupendranath Basu warned that "the canonization of a bureaucracy" would mean perpetual tutelage; "an increasing dead weight on the soul of India, it would be a curse to civilization and a blot on humanity".

C.R. Das was scathing in his attack on "a system of benevolent despotism carried on through a self-willed bureaucracy". India no longer wanted trustees or guardians, utilitarian benefactors or evangelical soul-savers. Indian forbearance was strained to breaking-point. Despotism, however self-sacrificing and self-critical, was bound to be helpless and capricious, nervous and irresponsible. It was often inspired by panic because it could not be sure and was out of touch with public opinion. Indians would rather be governed by a cold, soulless, representative machinery than be fantastically treated to fits of concession and oppression by the best-meaning bureaucracy in the world. India had to develop a political personality of its own. "Without overrating itself, a people does not arrive at knowledge of itself at all." All government without the consent of the governed is, as Swift said, the very definition of slavery.

In his Presidential Address to the Congress in 1922, C.R. Das challenged the whole political philosophy of the bureaucracy — the maintenance of law and order on the part of the government and an attitude of passive obedience and non-resistance on the part of the subject. "But was not that the political philosophy of every English king from William the Conqueror to James II? And was not that the political philosophy of the Romanoffs, the Hohenzollerns and of the Bourbons? And yet freedom has come, where it has come, by disobedience of the very laws which were proclaimed in the name of the law and order. Where the Government is arbitrary and despotic and the fundamental rights of the people are not recognized, it is idle to talk of law and order."

It was Gandhi's unique merit that in his combination of different methods, in his appeal to the British conscience, in his criticisms of the political theory of British imperialism, in his declaration of no confidence in the system, he was able to get down to fundamentals. He spoke in terms of Indian thought in accents of ringing sincerity and the deepest integrity that revealed courage, compassion, a patience born of strength and a purity that came through suffering. "An Englishman", he told C.F. Andrews, "never respects you till you stand up to him. Then he begins to like you. He is afraid of nothing physical; but he is very mortally afraid of his own conscience if ever you appeal to it, and show him to be in the wrong. He does not like to be rebuked for wrong-doing at first; but he will think it over, and it will get hold of him and hurt him till he does something to put it right." Gandhi did not directly appeal to British qualities of fair-play and justice; he took these for granted and went straight to the point. While his imperial antagonists preached Christianity and his Indian critics talked Hinduism, he practised both and thus confounded those who thought they could unnerve or undermine him. Similarly, he put his finger on the central assumptions of the four doctrines.

Only individuals could be trustees, not nations. No man loses his freedom except through his own weakness. A despotic government is maintained by the passive acquiescence of the people, by a hypnotic spell that has to be stoutly resisted. "Even the most despotic government cannot stand except for the consent of the governed, which consent is often forcibly procured by the despot. Immediately the subject ceases to fear the despotic force, his power is gone." "The state represents violence in a concentrated and organized form. The individual has a soul, but as the state is a soulless machine, it can never be weaned from violence to which it owes its very existence." A votary of non-violence cannot subscribe to the utilitarian formula. "He will strive for the greatest good of all and die in the attempt to realize the ideal. . . . The greatest good of all inevitably includes the good of the greatest number, and therefore, he and the utilitarian will converge in many points of their career, but there does come a time when they must part company and even work in opposite directions. The utilitarian to be logical will never sacrifice himself. The absolutist will even sacrifice himself." As to guardianship, "there is no room for patronage among equals" and "there will never be equality so long as one feels inferior or superior to the other".

Imperial domination must be replaced by a partnership on equal terms, a partnership that should not be 'subjection' in glorified language, like a relationship between a giant and a dwarf that was utilized for the exploitation of the other races of the earth. The British Empire, felt Gandhi, was an empire only because of India. A new concept of Indo-British partnership must emerge, "giving the promise of a world set free from exploitation". Every country was entitled to freedom without any question of its fitness or otherwise. "The doctrine of fitness to govern is a mere eye-wash. Independence means nothing more or less than getting out of alien control." Real partnership must be "no cloak for rulership".

As to evangelical Christians, the least Gandhi could say was to doubt if they had benefited India and the most he could say was that "they have repelled India from Christianity and placed a barrier between Christian life and Hindu or Musalman life. When I go to your scriptures I do not see the barrier raised, but when I see a missionary I find that barrier rising up before my eyes. I want you to accept this testimony from one who was for a time susceptible to those influences. . . . I have a definite feeling that if you want us to feel the aroma of Christianity, you must copy the rose. The rose irresistibly draws people to itself, and the scent remains with them. Even so, the aroma of Christianity is subtler even than the rose and should, therefore, be imparted in an even quieter, and more imperceptible manner, if possible."

Further, the Christian imperialists had much to learn from Indian religious thought and ethics. No one chained a slave without chaining himself. And no nation kept another in subjection without itself turning into a subject nation. Imperialism was resulting in the "brutalization of human beings". "I know that people who voluntarily undergo a course of suffering raise themselves and the whole of humanity, but I also know that people who become brutalized in their desperate efforts to get victory over their opponents or to exploit weaker nations or weaker men not only drag down themselves but mankind also. And it cannot be a matter of pleasure to me or anyone else to see human nature dragged in the mire. If we are all sons of the same God and partake of the same divine essence, we must partake of the sin of every person whether he belongs to us or to another race."

To deny a nation its freedom was not to withhold a gift, but to deprive it of its birthright. Indians, too, had to suffer and sacrifice themselves in the attempt to gain their liberty. The aim must be a "partnership between two races, the one having been known for its manliness, bravery, courage and its unrivalled power of organization, and the other an ancient race possessing a culture perhaps second to none, a continent in itself". Such a partnership, as that between the Romans and the Greeks, "cannot but result in mutual good and be to the benefit of mankind". Gandhi appealed to a gathering of Etonians not to follow slavishly, when they grew up, the footsteps of earlier empire builders like Wellesley, Metcalfe, Canning, Elgin, Dufferin, Lansdowne, Curzon and Irwin and many others, but instead "to make a unique contribution to the glory of your nation, by emancipating it from its sin of exploitation, and thus contribute to the progress of mankind".

He told a group of Oxford dons: "The long and short of it is that you will not trust us. Well, give us the liberty to make mistakes. If we cannot handle our affairs today, who is to say when we will be able to do so? I do not want you to determine the pace. Consciously or unconsciously you adopt the role of divinity. I ask you for a moment to come down from that pedestal. Trust us to ourselves, I cannot imagine anything worse happening than is happening today, a whole humanity lying prostrate at the feet of a small nation."

At a much wider gathering in London, Gandhi asked, "Who is it that can say that you have conferred benefits on India? We or you? . . . A series of men, Naoroji, Pherozeshah Mehta, Ranade, Gokhale — who used to dote on you, who were proud of British contact and of the benefits conferred by your civilization – do you know that they are all agreed in saying that you have on the whole done harm to India? When you go, you will have left us an impoverished and emasculated people, and the shades of all who loved you will ask, what have you done during these years of tutelage? You must realize that we cannot afford to have doorkeepers at your rate of wages, for you are no better than doorkeepers and a nation with an income of two pence a day per head cannot pay those wages. . . . Well, was it not Sir Henry Campbell Bannerman who said that good government is no substitute for self-government? You, who are past masters in making mistakes, you, who in the language of Lord Salisbury know the art of blundering through to success, will you not give us the liberty of making mistakes? . . . The iron has entered the soul of thousands of men and women who are impatient of alien control. We are impatient to gain this freedom, with your help, if you will, without your help if we must."

Gandhi challenged all the assumptions underlying trusteeship, guardianship, utilitarianism and evangelicalism. He also stressed that the British imperialists were not bad but the victims of an evil system, "so that the system must be destroyed and not the individual". He believed in the English despite the system, not because of it. "I believe in the good faith of England to the extent that I believe in the good faith of human nature. I believe that the sum total of the energy of mankind is not to bring us down but to lift us up, and that is the result of the definite, if unconscious, working of the law of love." To Gandhi "we are all tarred with the same brush; we are all members of the vast human family. I decline to draw any distinctions. I cannot claim any superiority for Indians. We have the same virtues and the same vices."

Gandhi was able to appeal to the British sense of guilt as well as the Indian sense of shame rather than to British or Indian pride. He challenged British imperialism not on utilitarian but on moral grounds. To him the system was *adharma,* devoid of any principle of moral authority or justification. The basic weakness of utilitarianism, in his eyes, was that it seemed to be a glorified power doctrine founded on a subtle form of violence. By talking the language of results, it led to a carelessness of the means, even an indifference to them. It could be invoked against notions of natural law and natural rights because it lent to factual considerations the emotive force of cherished values and matters of principle. Gandhi in his *Hind Swaraj* adopted a standpoint in regard to utilitarianism which was taken, to a lesser extreme, by Keynes in *Two Memoirs.*

Keynes regarded utilitarianism as "the worm which has been gnawing at the insides of modern civilization and is responsible for its present moral decay. We used to regard the Christians as the enemy, because they appeared as the representatives of tradition, convention, and hocus-pocus. In truth it was the Benthamite calculus, based on over-valuation of the economic criterion, which

was destroying the quality of the popular Ideal."
The final *reductio ad absurdum* of Benthamism was
Marxism, a brutal and illegitimate descendent of the
early proponents of State philanthropy and State
patronage.

Benthamites and Marxists could employ their brands
of utilitarianism to sanctify different forms of
imperialism, as they could also be used in support of
various types of nationalism. Just as Whiggery started
back in horror at its spiritual offspring when it became
the official creed of the revolted American colonies, so
too imperialists recoil with shock when they find that
their former theories are mirrored in the policies and
doctrines of triumphant nationalists. The new ruling
class in the Indian subcontinent achieves its ends by a
utilitarian appeal to results. When in power, the original
leaders of the national movement regarded themselves
as the natural trustees of popular welfare and behaved
at times like Platonic guardians of the masses in need of
guidance. The religious evangelicalism of the past is now
paralleled by a secular gospel of liberal, democratic
socialism or by more unfamiliar and hybrid creeds.

The role of trustees and of guardians and of
missionaries is attractive to every élite in power, to
every ruling class under modern representative
government as under authoritarian regimes. How to
justify the acquisition and the possession of power
and what to do with power when justified are the
problems that face every new government in the

presence of an alert and vocal electorate or even of an acquiescent but potentially restless population. It is a great tribute to the methods and ideas of Gandhi that although he would not have approved of all the policies and doctrines of the new ruling class in India, it is possible to appeal to its sense of guilt as well as of shame, of betrayal as well as of failure, when worthy ends are pursued by questionable methods or when worthy means are employed to achieve doubtful ends. This is especially valuable in the face of the authoritarian utilitarianism of ruthless Benthamite planners or Marxist dogmatists as well as the sectarian demands of religious fanatics.

It would be misleading to regard the political doctrines of British imperialism and especially of Benthamite utilitarianism as the direct cause of the political doctrines of Indian nationalism or of the present Indian government. Elements of trusteeship, guardianship, utilitarianism and even of missionary zeal can all be found in Indian political thought and tradition, although there are other and more dominant elements in Indian as in British thought and life. Behind all the failures and successes of the political theories of British imperialism lay the fact that the system they justified was a despotism and that the men who administered it were alien. Had the British settled down in the country and played the part of the Manchus in China, many of their theories and doings would have lasted longer and taken deeper root in Indian life, with the Indian genius for assimilation. Foreign rule could not be a proper, let alone a permanent, cure for the varied ills of Indian society that alone made foreign rule possible. The last thing that the imperialists thought of doing was to stimulate the growth of an organic political structure or a system of political ideas congenial to the new renaissance of ancient Indian civilization. Further, no material benefits, no cultural influences, could outweigh the wrong of a relationship that lamed a people's will, insulted its self-respect and doomed it to passivity and political slavery. And yet, it was Indian weakness, not English strength, that made English paramountcy possible. That the English solution to the problem of imperial government was worse than any alternative solution available to them in the context of their ideas or of the circumstances is not certain.

It was in any case inevitable that, in Chinese terms, the mandate of Heaven would be withdrawn when it was challenged, and not the least proof of that inevitability was the persisting doubt and the strains of scepticism of the English about their imperial mission in India. Meanwhile, the imperialists had unwittingly brought into Indian society a new vitality and strength lacking in Moghul India, had unintentionally initiated the vigorous political awakening of the masses and the emergence of a new middle class which has been compared to the Roman equestrian order, "with the means and the will to check the power of the government". By the very application of their doctrines, the trustees, the guardians, the utilitarians and the evangelicals brought about their own downfall, leaving behind them scattered traces of their thought and vocabulary.

APPENDIX

UTILITARIANISM AND EMPIRE

The role of the British in India has sometimes been compared to that of the Romans in their empire. Both were historic instruments of cultural diffusion and political unification. But these similarities cannot do as much credit to the British Empire as its overriding dissimilarity in one essential respect: the general sense of guilt, of recurring moral doubt about the validity of the imperial mission. As long as the sense of guilt was irrepressible, the urge for self-justification was also inescapable. To the subject peoples, the insistence on moral idealism rather than on material advantage, on the part of their conquerors, appeared to be either self-deception or hypocrisy. But to the ruling race, the question "What right here gives its sanction to might?" could be answered, in all sincerity, in terms of "their solemn duty to serve the interests of the ruled", to protect their subjects from their own weaknesses and from the designs of ambitious men. Such an answer at least shows that those who propounded it were sufficiently developed morally to admit that there was a question to be answered.

If the Roman Empire unintentionally spread Christianity more than paganism, the British can be said

to have disseminated the gospel of utilitarianism rather
than of Christianity. But in practice it was a doctrine
with two faces; utilitarian considerations are not
necessarily the basis of representative democracy and
liberal capitalism. They can be equally employed to
justify authoritarian regimes and enlightened despotism.
Interference with the negative liberties of others can be
justified not only in terms of idealistic metaphysics, of
higher selves and real wills, but also by reference to their
own real and long-term interests of which they may be
unaware. Once, however, this utilitarian element enters
into the notion of liberty, this danger of justifiable
coercion arises. It could then be argued that a man may
(or must) be trained how to choose and how to know
what his needs and all his wants are. More generally and
plausibly, an imperialist could claim that he can protect
the liberties of his subjects better than they could do by
themselves or through representatives of their own race
and nationality. It is not, therefore, surprising that the
nationalist has to retaliate against a theory of paternal
utilitarianism with an assertion of transferred natural
rights, by claiming that the sanctity of individual
personality and of national status are one and the same.

The paternal element in British utilitarianism easily
lent itself to imperial ends as well as to theories of
self-justification. Imperial experience in its turn further
weakened and sometimes destroyed the feeling for the
liberal element in utilitarianism. To Milner, both the
British Constitution and the party system were
"antiquated and bad", as they undermined the

effectiveness of positive government. Fitzjames Stephen, who was more Hobbesian than even Bentham or Austin, could claim that John Stuart Mill had perverted the pure doctrine of his father by yoking it to popular liberalism. The task of government, according to him, was to impose the ideal of happiness of a gifted ruling class upon a passive majority that had to be saved from its own anarchic tendencies. But such ideas, like the earlier nabobs and latter-day sahibs who returned to England, were strangers in the land of their birth. In an era of expanding trade, the rising power of the middle classes was hostile to bureaucratic government. Liberalism at home could thus coexist with benevolent despotism abroad. The Empire represented a compromise between conflicting principles, summed up by Disraeli as *Imperium et Libertas.*

In the resultant attitude to empire, we can identify diverse elements. There was the noble 'Roman' element, the desire to maintain the rule of law and to cherish the *pax Britannica,* the sheer concern for good government in the most mundane sense but on a grand scale. Secondly, there was the racial element, the doctrine of the chosen people, the belief that the English were divinely appointed to bear the white man's burden for the benefit of those beyond the pale. "Progress and reaction", declared Disraeli, "are but words . . . all is race." This notion was combined with the Darwinian doctrine of the survival of the fittest and later on was popularized by Kipling. Thirdly, there was the aggressive or 'Prussian' element, the pride in military power, the requirement of

docility in the ruled, the justification of occasional
severity to crush opposition to the regime. This element
was rather thin but it did exist, as was shown, for
instance, by some of the arguments used to justify
General Dyer's action at Amritsar in 1919. Finally,
there was the Radical or nonconformist element of
atonement and expiation. Bright argued that if the
British were willing to prepare for the time when India
would have her own government, they would be
endeavouring "to make amends for the original crime
upon which much of our power in India is founded, and
for the many mistakes which have been made by men
whose intentions have been good".

Such attitudes to empire are hardly susceptible to
more exact definition; fortunately we are on firmer
ground when we come to the principles and theories of
imperial government. I have already mentioned in passing
the predominantly utilitarian character of the British
approach to empire; but when we examine this more
closely we can distinguish, I think, four distinct strands:
the Burkean doctrine of imperial trusteeship; the
Benthamite theory of state activity as propagated and
modified by the two Mills; the Platonic conception of a
ruling élite that would act as wise guardians; and the
Evangelical zeal to spread the Christian gospel so as to
save the souls of a perversely unresponsive people. All
four theories formed part of the English intellectual
climate of their time; all four, when transplanted to
India, displayed the same mixture of good and bad in
practice. The noble Burkean doctrine could be distorted,

especially at times of stress, by the Prussian element: the trustees, in fact, could sometimes become overbearing. The Benthamite doctrine could degenerate into Hobbesian coercion and concentration of power; but it was also sublimated by the Roman element into a theory of legal unification and state philanthropy. The Platonic doctrine was at times enhanced by a Whig belief in liberalism and progress: but it was also perverted by the racial element in British imperialism into the concept of a chosen people. The Evangelical doctrine gave rise to many religious fears and resentments among Indians; but it was fortunately counterbalanced by the Christian notion of atonement which required that a believer should be concerned with his own sins as much as with saving the souls of others.

The Burkean doctrine of trusteeship was essentially conservative. It usually went with a reverence for the past, a distrust of theory. It meant in practice an unwillingness to trust the subjects to do anything for themselves. The trustees assumed that they alone knew and loved the real India. What began as an underestimation of the new Indian intelligentsia became in time a fierce phobia. If the Burkean doctrine appeared in course of time to be a formula borrowed from the missionary by the politician to cover up the naked fact of domination, this was really because of the growing sense of alienation between rulers and ruled. For this reason the theory of trusteeship must eventually break down, whilst providing inspiration and a private moral code to the finest spirits among the wielders of power.

When we turn to the Benthamites, we find that they also had a large forward-looking conception of what they were trying to achieve. Benthamite utilitarianism was not merely responsible for many social reforms and material benefits; it also introduced a spirit of scepticism and curiosity, of innovation and initiative, a spirit that was badly needed in a decadent and apathetic society. The utilitarian doctrine, however, had little use for representative institutions. Could an imperial authority, administered from afar through alien officials, be properly aware of the wants and interests of the people? Was it not too optimistic to assume a constant identity of interests between rulers and ruled? These questions arise because an empire could never achieve in practice the unity and social cohesion that might exist within a nation. But the utilitarians made the exercise of absolute power subject to self-imposed rules, so that it ceased to be arbitrary and became dependable. A bridge was thus provided between the power impulse of colonial administrations and Burke's exacting notion of moral responsibility. Whilst the trustee took pride in his intentions and his sense of responsibility, the utilitarian relied on results and his sense of achievement.

It was Jowett who showed how the Platonic doctrine of guardianship could be applied to India. The advantages of the Platonic model were not only propagandist but also practical. It helped the ruling class and the ruling race to believe in its mission and its destiny. It facilitated the education and the discipline of the civil service. Moreover it fostered standards of fairness within the framework of a system that took despotic power and prestige for granted. If the guardians were aloof, so were their willing and unwilling wards alike. If they became an exclusive caste, they could claim to be following the example of the Hindus. Apart from anything else, they did not mind – in fact almost took pride in – being disliked. The Platonic model was sustained by the comforting belief that the British guardians could never be replaced from among a people who were looked upon as 'eternal Peter Pans'. Instinctive race prejudice was raised to the status of a doctrine. Every Indian was regarded as incorrigibly corrupt or inherently inefficient or both.

Guardianship was in itself a grand ideal in terms of its own assumptions. These were, however, naturally unacceptable to a mature if corrupt civilization. In any case, it was extremely difficult for the best of guardians to serve two masters, to fulfil equally his duties to India and to England. As Sir Bartle Frere saw, there was something wrong about a policy which treated imperial subjects "as at best *in statu pupillari,* to be ruled, taught and perhaps petted, but to be excluded from all real power or influence . . . and to be governed . . . according to our latest English notion of what is best for them".

Burkean trustees, Platonic guardians, even Benthamite utilitarians from the very beginning, sought and received an additional sanction in the supernatural. British rule in India had to be seen as an act of providence rather than a mere accident of history. Evangelicalism gave a sense of urgency, an intensity of zeal and a largeness of scope to British imperialism in India. Its real weakness was that it assumed that all the giving and serving were on one side and all the receiving and the need were on the other. The evangelical belief that legislation was powerless to change human nature was, of course, an antidote against utilitarian legalism. The faith of the evangelicals in Anglicization undermined the Burkean veneration for Indian tradition. Their view of education as a universal panacea counteracted to some extent the hierarchical notion of a Platonic élite. It is a paradox that evangelicalism, which took the initiative in the West for the physical emancipation of slaves, was able at the same time to provide in the East the justification for the political enslavement of freemen.

The interaction between the four doctrines is too subtle and complex to be reduced to any simple scheme. There were affinities as well as contradictions among all of them, but collectively they had continuing force and even a strange unity. It was natural that trusteeship should appeal especially to the British Parliament, utilitarianism to the imperial government in India, guardianship to the civil service, and evangelicalism to non-official educational bodies. More generally, Burke provided a moral code, Bentham a programme, Plato an attitude of mind, and Wilberforce a transcendental sanction. All these were somehow needed if the feeling for principle was to come to terms with the facts of power, whilst reason had to serve as well as to restrain emotion. The four chief doctrines produced the strange result that the imperial rulers, who could not put their trust in princes or in politicians, unintentionally helped to democratize India, while adhering to their own polite form of autocratic government. All four doctrines were held with the utmost sincerity; this the cynics, who claim superior honesty, can deny only at the expense of truth. The apologists, who claim superior knowledge, can deny only at the expense of justice that all four doctrines were abused as well as misinterpreted.

The four doctrines do not go to make a grand symphony. There were too many discordant notes, too many jerks and surprises. If there was a symphony, it sounded at times as if it could have been by Beethoven and at other times by Bartok — in any case, it was a form of music to which few Indians could respond. At different times the four doctrines were challenged by Indian nationalists, but it was Gandhi's unique merit that in his attack on the political theory of British imperialism he was able to get down to fundamentals and appeal to the British conscience. He argued that only individuals could be trustees, not nations. The utilitarian, to be logical, could never sacrifice himself. As for guardianship, there was "no room for patronage among equals". Finally, he argued that evangelicalism only produced in India a revulsion from Christianity.

Gandhi was able to appeal to the British sense of guilt as well as to the Indian sense of shame. He challenged British imperialism not on its own terms but on his own. The system was condemned by him as *adharma,* a Sanskrit term meaning 'devoid of moral or religious justification'. Utilitarianism, in his eyes, was merely a glorified power doctrine founded on a subtle form of violence. By talking the language of results, it led to a carelessness of the means. It could be invoked against notions of natural law and natural rights because it lent to factual considerations the emotive force of cherished values.

Yesterday's imperialists may feel a sense of outrage when they find their own former theories mirrored today in the policies and doctrines of triumphant nationalism. The new ruling class achieves its ends by a utilitarian appeal to results. The leaders of the national movement, now in power, regard themselves as the natural trustees of popular welfare and behave at times like Platonic guardians of the masses in need of guidance. The religious evangelicalism of the past is now paralleled by a secular gospel of liberal, democratic socialism. The role of trustees and guardians, of benefactors and missionaries, is attractive to almost every ruling class under modern representative government as under authoritarian regimes. The British had unwittingly brought into Indian society a new vitality and strength lacking in Moghul India. They had unintentionally initiated the vigorous political awakening of the masses and the emergence of a new middle class. By the very application of their doctrines, they brought about their own downfall; and in due course the British Empire in India had to come to an end.

The Third Programme   *The Listener*
B.B.C., London   March 24, 1960

THE JEWEL IN THE LOTUS

Edited by RAGHAVAN IYER

The Jewel in the Lotus is a comprehensive collection of chants, invocations and intimations from the world's religions and mystical traditions. Its breadth, depth and universality will appeal to the general reader as well as to practitioners of meditation. It will bring joy and inspiration, solace and regeneration, to occasional as well as regular users.

605 pp. Sewn, softbound

THE PLATONIC QUEST

By E. J. URWICK

The Platonic Quest by E.J. Urwick is a path-breaking interpretation of Plato's *Republic* that weaves together Socratic-Platonic teachings and classical Indian concepts. Urwick portrays the social structure of the *Republic* as a holistic vision. Breaking the scholastic interpretations of earlier philologists and later positivists, giving full measure to the profound and puzzling themes of the *Republic*, Urwick also shows the coherence of the dialogue as a living testament to the human potential for spiritual wisdom. By integrating elements from humanity's ancient heritage, he restores depth and meaning to the Platonic quest while intimating its promise for the future. The book is enriched by an introductory chapter on the Platonic dialectic and an epilogue on *anamnesis* by Professor Raghavan Iyer.

xxxiv + 262 pp. Sewn, softbound

PARAPOLITICS
Toward the City of Man

By RAGHAVAN IYER

"*Parapolitics* is a work of large-scale political theory. The book is a very fluent and readable piece of work ... unusual in trying to combine the concern of existential psychology with the more conventional concerns of traditional political theory."

The Times Literary Supplement

"Erudition is united with wisdom in this stimulating work." *Journal of Politics*

"The heart of the book is the attempt to sketch a foundation for a global society of the future ... an ambitious and original undertaking." *Choice*

"*Parapolitics* is certainly something that is needed today." Arne Naess, University of Oslo

"A powerful, well-written and important book." James Joll, London School of Economics

"A unique plan of meditation for all politicians, political theorists and philosophers." Robert Rein'l, Arizona State University

"It is a first-class reappraisal of the classic problems of politics and a beautiful attempt to indicate some new roads to breaking the deadlock of our time." Helio Jaguribe De Mattos, Brazil

x + 381 pp. Hardbound

INSTITUTE OF WORLD CULTURE

DECLARATION

To explore the classical and renaissance traditions of East and West and their continuing relevance to emerging modes and patterns of living

To renew the universal vision behind the American Dream through authentic affirmations of freedom, excellence and self-transcendence in an ever-evolving Republic of Conscience

To honour through appropriate observance the contributions of men and women of all ages to world culture

To enhance the enjoyment of the creative artistry and craftsmanship of all cultures

To deepen awareness of the universality of man's spiritual striving and its rich variety of expression in the religions, philosophies and literatures of humanity

To promote forums for fearless inquiry and constructive dialogue concerning the frontiers of science, the therapeutics of self-transformation, and the societies of the future

To investigate the imaginative use of the spiritual, mental and material resources of the globe in the service of universal welfare

To examine changing social structures in terms of the principle that a world culture is greater than the sum of its parts and to envision the conditions, prospects and possibilities of the world civilization of the future

To assist in the emergence of men and women of universal culture, capable of continuous growth in non-violence of mind, generosity of heart and harmony of soul

To promote universal brotherhood and to foster human fellowship among all races, nations and cultures

The Institute of World Culture, founded on July 4, 1976 *(Bicentennial)*, has launched influential publications to generate a continuing inquiry into the prospects and possibilities, the conditions and requirements, of the world civilization of the future. Current publications include analyses of contemporary social structures, contributions to philosophic and literary thought, as well as classic reprints from Plato, ancient Indian psychology, Edward Bellamy and Leo Tolstoy. They invite the reader to rethink and renew a vital sense of participation in the global inheritance of humanity and the emerging cosmopolis.

1407 Chapala Street
Santa Barbara, CA 93101

The CGP emblem identifies this book as a production of Concord Grove Press, publishers since 1975 of books and pamphlets of enduring value in a format based upon the Golden Ratio. This volume was typeset in Bodoni Bold, and Press Roman Italic, printed, Smyth sewn and doubly bound by Sangam Printers. A list of publications can be obtained from Concord Grove Press, P.O. Box 959, Santa Barbara, California 93102, U.S.A.